There Are Demons In The Sea

Preaching The Message Of The Miracles

Cycle B

Richard Carl Hoefler

CSS Publishing Company, Inc., Lima, Ohio

THERE ARE DEMONS IN THE SEA

Revised Edition 2002

For more information about CSS Publishing Company resources, visit our website at www.csspub.com or e-mail us at custserv@csspub.com or call (800) 241-4056.

ISBN 0-7880-1917-1
                                    PRINTED IN U.S.A.

Dedicated
to my parents
in celebration of their
sixtieth wedding anniversary

Table Of Contents

Introduction

The miracles can be understood only in relationship to the cross and the Resurrection, for it is from this perspective the Gospel writers recorded them. The Evangelists told the stories of the miracles not to commemorate a deceased and defeated teacher and friend, but to proclaim a living Savior and victorious Lord.

Jesus came to his ministry accepting as his first task the role of *herald* proclaiming the coming of the Kingdom of God; but he came also as *hero* to establish and make possible a kingdom of God's rule here on earth.

In the decisive battle against evil, Christ died on the cross; in his death he was not victim, but victor. From this death he was raised to glory and the rule of God was established over all the earth.

Jesus as warrior is particularly apparent in the Gospel According to Mark. The concern of Mark was not so much with what Jesus said and taught, as with who he was and what he did. For Mark, Jesus was the Son of God sent into the world to redeem the world, to rescue the world from the domination of the demonic and restore God's rule.

Evil powers held God's creation captive and would not give up without a struggle. Therefore Christ came as a warrior to do battle. He came not as a political king with might to drive out the Romans from his beloved homeland, which many of his fellow Jews desired; but he came as a Suffering Servant who with meekness exercised the power of God driving the evil forces out of this world and defeating Satan, the chief enemy of God.

Christ came to set God's people free — free from ways of disobedience, disease, and death. Therefore, each of the miracle events was a battle won, and Jesus, the conquering Son of God, advanced closer to his ultimate victory in the event of the cross and Resurrection.

Christ as conqueror does not rule out compassion as an element in the healing miracles of Jesus. He was concerned and cared for the person who came seeking his help. His concern, however,

7

went beyond compassion. His desire was not simply to heal but to make whole, which meant that the person's relationship to God be re-established. Those who benefited from his healing power were cured not only *from* something but *for* something. The end of the experience was not just restored health, but return to fellowship with God the creator.

The miracle events were not "faith-healings" in our contemporary understandings of the term. Faith was not the cause of the miracle, but resulted from it. Therefore, the miracles were not presented as examples of people's ability to believe, but they were signs and symbols pointing to God's gift of freedom and faith — freedom from the demonic and evil powers of this world, and faith, a new relationship with God.

In the discussions which follow, this is the viewpoint from which each miracle will be studied. They are events, battles in the war of God against rebellion within his creation.

Such an approach may seem too mythological for many who desire to understand the miracles. Mark, however, thought mythologically, and if we are to discover the meaning and message he wishes to convey, we must accept his thought form.

In the following discussions of the miracle stories, the issue will not be the factuality of these events but their *reality*. An event told as story is real when we can be drawn into the story, identify with it, and be changed by it. Such are the accounts of the miracles as recorded by Mark. They are real. When we listen as Mark tells them they become alive and their messages speak to us where we are with a meaning that is personal and practical. In these records of what Christ once did we are confronted by the Christ who first worked these acts of wonder, and we discover he is even now working a wonder-inspiring change in us. The issue, therefore, is not did the miracles happen then, but will they happen now, in us?

Miracle 1

The Gordian Knot

A Man Possessed By An Evil Spirit

Luke 4:31-37 *(parallel text)*

Henry David Thoreau made the profound observation that most people lead lives of quiet desperation. This miracle story centers about a man who shocked a synagogue congregation one Sabbath morning with his *noisy* desperation.

Jesus had come to Capernaum with his disciples and on the next day, which was the Sabbath, he went as was his custom to the synagogue to speak.

What he said that day impressed the people. It was fresh, plain, and practical — so different from the formal and musty teachings of the local scribes. Both the substance of what he said and the manner in which he said it had a ring of authority. The people were amazed at his teachings. They sensed that something new was happening and that it had something to do with the coming of the Kingdom.

Then it happened. A shriek split the holy atmosphere of the synagogue. Jesus stopped speaking. The man who had screamed was hurled as if by unseen hands into the midst of the astonished congregation. He tossed about upon the floor in a violent fit. The people were dumbfounded. They could not believe what they were witnessing.

"What do you want with us, Jesus of Nazareth? Are you here to destroy us? I know who you are: you are God's holy messenger!"

The stunned congregation looked about to see who was shouting forth these words. The voice seemed to come from the convulsing figure on the floor; yet it sounded more like a chorus of demons shouting forth from hell.

Jesus scorned this weird profession of faith. "Be quiet!" he shouted. "Come out of that man!" With that, the frenzied figure on the floor shook and quivered all the more and uttered another ear-piercing scream. Then a silence like the hush of death. The evil spirit had come out of the man and the whole ghastly incident was over as suddenly as it had begun.

At first the congregation was speechless; then, still too overcome with shock to speak out loud, they whispered to one another, "What is this? This man gives orders to the evil spirits and they obey him."

What a story! Alfred Hitchcock at his best could hardly create so suspenseful and spine-tingling a drama as that which was enacted on a quiet Sabbath morning in a little town tucked away on the shores of the Sea of Galilee.

So Jesus began his Galilean ministry. Despite the melodramatic aspects of its beginning, the incident most appropriately symbolizes his entire earthly ministry. He has shown himself Lord of both the synagogue and the Sabbath. Here, word and action, deed and doctrine, were dramatically forged together. He had taught with *authority*, and he had cast out evil spirits with *power*.

But most important of all, here our Lord had encountered the enemy he had come to destroy and he had held the day. Christ had won this initial battle against an advance guard, but the war had just begun. Therefore, our miracle story stands as sign and symbol of the exciting campaign our Lord is about to embark upon, and it entices us to a more detailed examination.

The Synagogue
Since the setting of the story is the synagogue at Capernaum, perhaps a brief word concerning the place and practices of the synagogue in Jewish life might be helpful before we examine the details of the miracle.

10

The origin of the synagogue is obscured in history. The only fact known for certain is that, as an institution, it became firmly established in the period of exile when it was impossible for devout Jews to attend the sacrifices of the Temple. The synagogue was a place for prayer, praising God by chanting the Psalms, and reading the Holy Scriptures; but most of all, it was a place for religious instruction.

In many ways what happened in the synagogue could be compared to what happens in modern Protestant worship services on Sunday morning, if we include the Sunday school instructional period. However, unlike in the average church today, there was no ordained clergy as we think of ordained ministers. There were leaders responsible for the administrative activities, the support and upkeep of the building, and the proper program for worship and instruction. There were also rulers of the synagogue, who served when necessary as leaders of the worship service.

Any male Israelite who was qualified to do so could lead the worship, read the Scriptures, and afterwards, if he desired, comment on the passage read. When the scribes were present they would generally teach, but in the small villages, particularly those a great distance from Jerusalem, the scribes were seldom residents.

In the early history of Christianity, the synagogue played a vital role, as it provided an established congregation and therefore a unique opportunity for Jesus, and later for Paul and his fellow missionaries, to teach. However, when the Gentiles began to join the church in numbers, more neutral places had to be found for presenting Christian teachings.

In this miracle story, Jesus had been asked by the leaders of the synagogue to teach. Today we might compare this to inviting in a guest preacher to deliver the Sunday morning sermon.

Amazed At The Way He Taught

Mark reports that when Jesus began to speak, the people who heard him were amazed at the way he taught.

There is not within our text, or within any of the New Testament, a description of the way Jesus taught, except that he taught with authority. We know nothing about the personal appearance of

11

our Lord, his use of gestures, the timbre of his voice, or his facial expression as he spoke his words. Lowries says, "When it is a question of personal authority, it is just these things that count."[1]

From the total lack of information concerning the personal appearance of our Lord, it seems obvious the Gospel writers felt the secret of Jesus' authority was to be found elsewhere. In our miracle story there is not even an account of the text or the content of the message Jesus spoke that day in the synagogue at Capernaum. This, according to Nineham, is typical of Mark, for he is always, "more interested in the effect of Jesus' teaching than in what was taught."[2]

On the basis of the total evidence of the Gospels, however, we can speculate concerning the manner of Jesus' teaching and get some insight into why the people were impressed and amazed at the *way* he taught.

In Luke 4:14-21, we have a record in more detail of Jesus teaching in the synagogue at Nazareth. On the basis of this and the other evidences in the New Testament of Jesus' teaching, we can create a picture reflecting some idea of his speaking style.

Scriptural

In Luke 4:17, we see that Jesus' teaching in the synagogue at Nazareth was scriptural. Luke records that he was handed the book of the prophet Isaiah. Jesus unrolled it and read. When he had finished reading, he sat down, taking the proper position for teaching or preaching in the synagogue, and began speaking to the people on the basis of the passage he had just read.

In Mark's account of Jesus' speaking in the synagogue at Capernaum, the reaction of the congregation was that "he wasn't like the teachers of the Law." By this they meant the scribes.

Lowrie is helpful here in pointing out that the scribes at the time of Jesus seldom spoke directly from the Scriptures, giving their own interpretations; rather, "The scribes recognized only authorities who were dead, or who based their decisions upon the opinion of ancient rabbis which ultimately appealed to the dead letter of Scripture. Here at least was a living and quickening authority."[3]

12

Practical

Jesus' teaching was personal, pointed, and practical. We can surmise this from the text he chose in the synagogue at Nazareth, which speaks of proclaiming good news to the poor, liberty to the captives, recovery of sight to the blind, freedom for the oppressed, and salvation for the people.

This spoke to where the people were. These were matters of great significance to the average person.

Lowrie says, "The key to Jesus' new teaching is that he came directly to the point, he personalized and made practical the Holy Scriptures."[4]

Great teaching and preaching is always bifocal, concerned both with the deeds of God and the needs of people. It is always a word directed toward the invasion of the common life to restore the broken relationship between the creator and the created, to establish a new option for human dignity and freedom, and to bring all creation to the fulfillment of its intended destiny.

So Jesus taught. And his penetrating insights into the practical concerns of the people amazed his listeners.

Prophetic

The teaching of Jesus was also prophetic. This means in the truest sense of the word "prophetic," that is, describing not the ability to predict the future but rather to *interpret the present*. For example, he concluded his sermon at the synagogue in Nazareth with the words, "This passage of scripture has come true today, as you heard it read."

Lane, referring to this aspect of Jesus' speaking style, writes that Jesus "confronted the congregation with the absolute claim of God upon their whole person. Jesus' teaching recalled the categorical demand of the prophets rather than scribal tradition."[5]

In another sense, however, Jesus did not speak like the prophets. There was a profound difference. As Sherman Johnson reminds us, "There is no record that Jesus ever said 'thus saith the Lord,' "[6] the phrase so characteristic of the prophets. These were men bidden by God to proclaim his message to the people. Often the prophets were reluctant to assume such a responsible task.

13

They felt unworthy to be voices used by God to speak his sacred words.

Not so with Jesus. He spoke of what the people had been told in the past and then he added, "But, I say unto you." He did not speak as one sent from God; he spoke as God, directly and spontaneously. Is it any wonder that the people who heard him were amazed that he taught and spoke with such absolute authority?

Fearlessly

One of the marks of gospel preaching is that it is seldom congenial with the thought and cultural habits of the times; rather it is in collision with them. It comes to question, to challenge things as they are, in an attempt to show people how God intended them to be. Therefore, preaching is met with resistance and counterattack.

This was true of Jesus' sermon in Luke 4:16-30, for he ended his sermon in the synagogue at Nazareth with a warning. He reminded his listeners how Israel had mistreated God's prophets in the past. Because of this God had turned his back upon his own people. He said, "And there were many lepers in Israel during the time of the prophet Elisha; yet not one of these was made clean, but one Naaman the Syrian."

That antagonized the congregation, for "Syrian" meant "Gentile," and that was a dirty word to the people of Israel. It was taken as a direct insult. Jesus implied that God had passed over the Jews and blessed the hated Gentile. So Luke says that the people were so angered, "They rose up, dragged Jesus out of town, and took him to the top of the hill ... to throw him over the cliff. But he walked through the middle of the crowd and went his way" (Luke 4:29, 30).

Jesus spoke in a way that was challenging. With courage he spoke of the change that must now occur because the Kingdom of God had come.

Picturesque

We can be certain that when he spoke, Jesus' ideas were well illustrated. He was a master craftsman at creating pictures in the minds of people that penetrated their memories, never to be forgotten. We

14

know this by the many parables he told which so dominate the content of his remembered teachings recorded in the New Testament.

He was a great storyteller. One of the reasons given by the narrative theologians for his preference for fishermen among his disciples is the fact that men of the sea have been in every age and culture commonly characterized as tellers of tales.

Whenever Jesus spoke, his style was picturesque, never abstract, involved, or complex. Perhaps that is why people were amazed when they heard him speak — they could understand him. Even when he talked of the profound issues of faith, he never presented them as mysterious truths to be thought through and then accepted; rather he presented them as penetrating pictures that once seen could not be rejected.

On the basis of these special passages recording his speaking in the synagogues at Nazareth and Capernaum, and of the total evidence of the Gospels, we can assume that the *way* he taught was scriptural, practical, prophetic, fearless, and picturesque. This should say something to all of us who face, in Joseph Sittler's words, *The Anguish of the Pulpit*. And for those of us who teach, it might present some interesting guidelines to our task.

Something Happened

Edward Schweizer gives perhaps the most profound interpretation of the *way* Jesus taught. He writes, "Jesus was distinguished from others not because he taught something completely different, but because he taught with such authority that things happened. Men were moved to action and sick persons were healed."[7]

Jesus spoke and *something happened*! That is the key to understanding the *way* Jesus taught, and that is the key to understanding how his teaching in the synagogue and his driving out of the evil spirit are related to form a single story. They both testify to the central, dominating factor of Christ's authority. He spoke. He acted. And something happened.

Man With An Evil Spirit

The man with an "evil spirit in him" causes great difficulty for many who read and study this passage.

A generation ago the popularity of W. P. Blatty's book, *The Exorcist*, and the movie based on it, helped make the idea of demons and possession by evil spirits seem less "outdated" to the sophisticated churchgoer than it had previously.

One newspaper, in referring to the movie, commented that it "created a national epidemic of hysteria and morbid curiosity unprecedented in modern times."[8] This is perhaps an overstatement; yet the word "curiosity" is to the point. Few today believe in demons and possession, but just about everybody is curious about the devil, demons, spirits, witchcraft, and the whole world of the occult. The persistence of Halloween over the years and its appeal to grownups as well as youngsters suggests in us all a certain natural fascination with the supernatural.

Demons

Interest in demons is as old as humankind. In fact, it is impossible for scholars to identify the origin of demons with any semblance of agreement.

Van der Loos says that "even the word demon (daimon) is uncertain." It is generally connected with the Greek verb meaning to "tear apart" or "divide."[9]

In some cultures demons are positive creatures. Minor gods are often referred to as demons even when they are considered to be friendly with humanity. People have also commonly believed demons to be the spirits of the dead, which have become ghosts and now come back to inhabit the earth for good as well as evil purposes.

In Judaism, however, where the gulf between deity and demons was at an early date widened, there was the accepted belief that demons were fallen angels. Van der Loos writes, "Just as the angel, as a good spirit, belonged to the realm of light, the Kingdom of God, so the demon belonged to the realm of darkness, the Kingdom of Satan."[10]

Alan Richardson observes that the Jewish world of the first century A.D. firmly believed in demons. And then he adds, "The Jews were well known as exorcists of demons throughout the ancient world and amongst themselves the power of exorcism was taken for granted."[11]

Richardson goes on to say, "Christianity conquered the other religions of the ancient world partly because of its success in casting out the fear of demons, and the Christians rapidly ousted the Jewish exorcists from their position of supremacy."[12]

Josephus, the Jewish historian, believed that Solomon received directly from God the secret of exorcism which gave the Jewish race its particular expertise in the art of driving out demons from the possessed. It was God's gift to his people in order that they might, in their covenant relationship to him, aid and heal humankind.

This was a gigantic task, for people lived in a haunted environment where no area was safe from demonic invasion and domination. The demons inhabited the dry sands of the desert, as well as the depths of the sea. They were feared most at night, but demons were known to attack a man at midday. No place — no time — no condition provided shelter or escape from the intense terror people experienced in the presence of the demonic loose in their world.

William Barclay comments that people in the time of Jesus "believed that the air was so full of them (demons) that it was not possible to insert the point of a needle into the air without touching one."[13]

Periods Of Concentration

History recounts certain periods of intensified interest and belief in the demonic. Just as *The Exorcist* created curiosity about the demonic, the fail of Jerusalem increased Jewish interest in the problem of personal possession by evil spirits.

Some scholars suggest that the intensity of belief in the demonic is in direct relationship to certain social, economic, and political conditions. When times are tough and tragedy follows greater tragedy, when life tumbles in and there are more questions than answers, belief in the demonic is increased. In periods of personal depression, when groups are persecuted or held down by economic or political forces, belief in demons becomes an opiate for the oppressed.

In the Middle Ages, for example, belief in the demonic ran rampant among the uneducated masses who were caught in a web of fear for their very existence. It was not only a time of appalling ignorance and plagues, but life was cheap and there was a complete disregard for the dignity of common humanity.

Even some of the great minds that helped ordinary people emerge from the darkness of the Middle Ages, like Luther for example, did not fully rise above a belief in the demonic. When flies flew over his books and distracted his attention, and rats disturbed his sleep at night, he accused demons of such deviltry.

Conclusions

Little is gained in arguing the reality of the demonic in the world, then or now. One thing is certain: Many people in all ages have believed in demons with terrified intensity.

For our understanding of the miracle story before us, it is important to note two things: First, in the days of Jesus there was a particularly strong wave of demonism within Palestine; and secondly, as H. Loewe points out, "Belief in demons was particularly strong in Galilee at the time of Jesus."[14] Therefore the setting and the time are right for an account of our Lord's casting out an evil spirit from a possessed man.

Relationship Of The Demonic To Disease

The view is commonly held that the writers of the New Testament were men of their age and therefore ascribed all physical illnesses and abnormalities to possession by evil spirits. Demon-possession thus is considered by many the term in the New Testament to describe insanity and extreme nervous disorders.

Today scholars are beginning to question this unqualified identification and see instead a distinction between the sick and the possessed. Lane, for example, takes the position that there is "a striking difference between the forms of address employed by the demoniacs and the titles used by ordinary sick individuals."[15]

This distinction between sickness and demonic possession is important so far as our miracle story is concerned, in that since this man is identified as one being possessed by an evil spirit, we have

18

here not just another "healing" miracle by Jesus but a *power encounter* of our Lord with an agent of Satan, his declared adversary and enemy.

The concept of encounter does not deny the possibility that "possession" was involved in all the healing miracles, but it clarifies the intent and the interest of Mark as he relates this story. He is not calling our attention to the ability of our Lord to heal a mentally disturbed man — even one suffering from severe insanity. Rather, Mark is presenting in this miracle account a sign that the battle begun in our Lord's temptation experience with Satan continues now as he opens his Galilean ministry.

Jesus Of Nazareth

The first words of the evil spirit are, "What do you want with us, Jesus of Nazareth?" In most cases, Jesus' being called "the Nazarene" simply reflects his humble origins. Occasionally the term is derogatory, as when Nathanael asks, "Out of Nazareth can any good come?"

Most scholars conclude that when the demon addressed our Lord "Jesus of Nazareth," he did not imply disdain but was simply using the title by which Jesus was generally known, particularly at this early stage of his ministry.

Are You Here To Destroy Us?

The question of the demon, "Are you here to destroy us?" sets the stage for the militant aspect of this miracle.

This is to be more than a mere exorcism, the drawing out of an unclean spirit. No customary equipment of the exorcists is used here; no magic formula, no sign of the cross, no prayers to God, just the sheer military command, "Be quiet, and come out of that man!" The words are used as a warrior would use his sword to pierce the enemy to the heart and destroy him.

Jesus envisioned his mission here on earth as a battle with the Evil One, Satan, the rebellious leader against God! Perhaps, to our sophisticated minds, belief in Satan smacks of "superstitious medievalism" and the "backward element" of religious belief in primitive societies. But before we completely reject belief in a personal

19

devil and the existence of the demonic, let us examine what the New Testament is witnessing to in this image of a personal devil, the Evil One, who invaded our world and holds us captive.

Origin Of Evil

The writers of Scripture assumed certain facts, a certain mindset and view of the universe in which they lived. From these derived a basic theology of the conflict between good and evil.

Briefly, this theology held that God had created the universe and that the earth was but a part of that total creation. In heaven there occurred a rebellion. One of the chief angels of God turned against him and was driven from heaven. This fallen angel assumed many names: Satan, the devil, Beelzebul, the Evil One.

The earth was created good. When man and woman were disobedient to God's will and also fell from their intended relationship to the Creator, the earth became vulnerable to the Evil One. It was as if a crack occurred in a protective sphere between earth and hell, and through this opening Satan slipped in to claim the earth for his domain. He invaded the entire realm of the earth; with the help of his demons, which were also fallen angels he had enticed to follow him, he held everything within his captive power.

The answer to the question of the origin of evil is to be found in the word "rebellion." Evil was born when the good which God created rebelled against him, defied him with willful disobedience, and turned back against God the goodness he had so freely given. Therefore, the power of evil comes, not from some original source built into the structure of existence, but from God's grace and goodness perverted to evil purposes. Evil takes what God gives as good and makes of it evil.

There is an ancient Chinese legend which tells of an army headed by two generals, Chon-Yu and Liang. At one decisive point in a war they were fighting, they ran out of arrows. They were certain they could defeat the enemy if only they could get a fresh supply of arrows.

So they devised a clever plan. They filled boats with straw soldiers, including a few real drummers and buglers, and sent the boats downstream toward the enemy. Hearing the sounds of drums and bugles, the enemy thought it was an attack and showered the straw figures and boats with arrows.

Chon-Yu and Liang, further down the river beyond the enemy, waited for the boats loaded with arrows and gathered the weapons for their own use.

This illustration breaks down at one important point: the arrows of God were not shot in anger at straw figures of the enemy; they were cupid-like arrows of love. They were not weapons, but gifts of grace. The main point of the comparative illustration does hold, however. Evil gets its power to do battle against *God* from *God himself*. Evil takes the goodness of God, perverts it into an evil force, and uses it against God. Therefore, the greater and more generous the grace of God, the greater the potential power of evil.

Apocalyptic

The great question dealt with in Holy Scripture is how long God will tolerate the existence of evil in his world and the dominant power the Evil One exercises over all the earth and humanity.

One answer was the apocalyptic view, which literally means "uncovered" or "revealed" view. It was a revelation of the future in which God would intervene by direct action, eliminate the hold of evil, and destroy sin, death, and the devil.

There were many theories of how God would bring about this action. Would he destroy the earth and create a new one? Would he give the whole thing up and destroy the earth with a mighty flood? Or would he establish his Kingdom rule on the earth? The most commonly held view was the latter. He would drive evil out, destroy the Evil One, and re-establish himself as ruler over all the land and over all the people. The kingdoms of this world would become the Kingdom of our God. The emphasis here was on the sovereign action of God in which he would assert his authority and bring everything into conformity with his will forever.

All the Gospel writers accepted that the powers of evil would not give up their hold over the world without a struggle. A bitter battle would therefore mark the coming of God's Kingdom here on earth, and people and nature would suffer, caught in the middle of the struggle.

Mark, in particular, viewed the ministry of Christ largely in terms of this battle between God and the evil powers of this world. Behind the evil powers stood the leader, often known to us as the devil, but mostly referred to by Mark as Satan or Beelzebul.

Hendriksen, when commenting on the question asked by the evil spirit, "Have you come to destroy us?" says that this "is best taken to mean 'have you come from heaven into the world ...' The demon, accordingly, is asking whether the very One who had come to *seek* and to *save* the lost had also come to destroy the demons...."[16]

Mark's answer is, "Yes." Salvation and the destruction of evil are one and the same act. The means by which Christ will save humanity is cross-shaped where God does battle against the forces of evil, where life defeats death, and where God emerges to reign victoriously.

The Holy One Of God

The confession made by the evil spirit, "you are the Holy One of God," or as some translations have it, "God's holy messenger" has been interpreted by scholars from two points of view.

Some, like Lane, see it not as a confession but as a weapon of attack. "This recognition-formula is not a confession," writes Lane, "but a defensive attempt to gain control of Jesus in accordance with the common concept of that day, that the use of the precise name of an individual or spirit would secure mastery over him."[17]

It was like the plot of the Grimm Brother's famous classic *Rumpelstiltskin*, in which the miller's daughter had to spin straw into gold to marry the king. Faced with this impossible task, she was about to give up when a little man appeared before her and said that he would spin the straw into gold, but she would have to promise to give him her firstborn son. She agreed.

When all the straw was spun into gold, the miller's daughter married her beloved, the king. Soon after the birth of their first son, the little man suddenly appeared and demanded what they had agreed upon, her firstborn son. She begged him to take instead all her riches and jewels, but he refused.

Seeing her desperate sorrow, the spinner of gold said, "I will give you one last chance to save your child. Guess my name, and if you do, then you may keep your baby."

For three days she searched the royal library, but to no avail. Then a messenger she had sent into the kingdom returned and said he had seen a strange sight. On a high hill where foxes and hares bid each other goodnight there was a little man dancing around a fire singing:

> *Oh, little thinks my royal dame,*
> *That Rumpelstiltskin is my name.*

The next day when the little man returned, she told him his name, Rumpelstiltskin. "The devil it is, the devil it is!" he screamed, and stamped his foot into the ground with such a fury that he split in two.

So in the days of our Lord, to know the name of a person gave strange powers over that person. With it one could control and even destroy the owner.

The most common interpretation of the demon's use of the name "the Holy One of God" is that the evil spirit is actually making a confession and therefore knows the "secret" of who Jesus is.

Van der Loos asks the obvious question, "How do demons know this secret?"[18] He reviews the various answers, such as that evil forces possessed supernatural knowledge which God himself had given them, or that demoniacs possessed clairvoyant and telepathic powers.

Van der Loos comes to the conclusion that "the various terms used by the demoniacs need not point to their having been equipped with supernatural knowledge."[19] His reason is that "the Holy One of God" was not synonymous with the title of Messiah. If the evil spirit had intended to confess Jesus before the synagogue congregation, he would have used the term "Messiah" which was at that time the title most associated with the "secret" of who Jesus was.

An important fact is that the title "the Holy One of God" is a rarely used one. As Moule points out, "In the New Testament it occurs, besides this place, only at Luke 4:34, parallel to this passage, and at John 6:69."[20] This would seem to indicate that its use does have a special significance, at least in the mind of Mark who records that detail of the story.

For our approach to the meaning of this miracle we will follow the interpretation represented by Lane. It supports the fact that the evil spirit did know who Jesus was and was therefore making a direct attack against the one God had sent to destroy the stronghold of Satan on earth. The title-name "the Holy One of God" was for the demon his "Rumpelstiltskin" to turn back the destruction.

This is not a confession of a believer ready to give up all and follow Jesus. This is not a supernatural being revealing a hidden secret. This is a demonic declaration — a declaration of war! The spirit is literally saying, "I know who you are! I know your name! And with it I will destroy you who desire to destroy us!"

Thus Mark records this miracle as a sign pointing to the cross where the final battle with the Evil One will be fought; he prepares the reader for the decisive victory of Christ who on the cross becomes the Christ of Glory, King of kings, and Lord of lords.

The Gordian Knot

What does the message of this miracle story mean for us today? It does not necessarily mean that we must believe in devils and demons, but it does demand that we recognize and confess the reality of evil both in our world and in ourselves.

We are a people possessed, possessed with desires that force us into deeds of disobedience against our God. We do not want to be what we are, and we are daily sorry for what we do. But our stubborn pride often prohibits us from falling down on our knees and humbly and completely surrendering ourselves unto the Lord. We hesitate to trust him all the way. We are afraid to place ourselves and our lives totally within his merciful hands.

So, again and again, like the possessed man in the miracle story, we fall to the floor of desperation, silently screaming within ourselves, struggling aimlessly and suffering endlessly from an enemy we refuse to recognize and have no strength to conquer.

24

Theologians of the Christian Church have long recognized the name of this enemy within us. Freudian psychology has analyzed and categorized the enemy within human personality.

Dostoyevski goes deeper perhaps than any when he apprehends with his artistic sensitivity the demonic in the human tragedy. He puts it most dramatically into the mouth of the demon who controls one of the Karamazov brothers: "Satan am I, and nothing human is foreign to me."

All these witnesses proclaim the single truth that the enemy who possesses us is our *self*. We are our own worst enemy. Self-centeredness, self-concern, self-preservation, self-pride, self, self, self; this is the enemy who possesses us and from which we can in no way set ourselves free.

We are like swimmers caught in a whirlpool; the harder we swim the more we are drawn into the center of the problem which is our *selves*!

Life waits all about us to give us new and good things. But we must search out, seek after, chase *nothing*! What we need is to surrender to our God who searches, seeks, and chases after us.

Every central story of the New Testament contains the same plot. It is the same account told again and again about the God who seeks out, reaches out, calls out to us, "I love you! I want you for my own! I have done all things for your salvation, for your freedom from all that possesses you."

Our Lord cries out to our demon-possessed self, "Be quiet! Come out of that man!" And the glorious good news of the gospel is that on the cross of Calvary the evil which is within us darkens the noonday sun, shakes the very earth in its death struggle, and comes out of us all.

One of the classic tales told around countless campfires during the fantastic rise and reign of Alexander the Great, conqueror of the world, was called "The Tale of the Gordian Knot."

The story begins: There existed a tiny Asian kingdom known as Phrygia. Its sole claim to fame rested on a special wagon in one of the courtyards of the capital city. The wagon was fastened to a yoke by an astonishing knot called the Gordian Knot. The wise men of the country prophesied that whoever untied the knot would conquer the world.

For a hundred years, the Gordian Knot had defied the herculean efforts of the cleverness of kings and the might of the strongest warriors. Then one day Alexander, the young king of Macedonia, journeyed to Phrygia to try his hand. When he arrived, the court-yard swarmed with curious spectators, everyone waiting in eager anticipation to see if this promising young ruler were equal to the task.

Alexander walked confidently into the courtyard. He carefully examined the knot. The suspense was electrifying. Then suddenly, to the surprise of all, Alexander swiftly withdrew his sword and with one mighty swinging blow cleanly sliced the knot in two!

For many of us life is a Gordian Knot. Troubles and problems entangle us, tying our lives into a snarled, meaningless mess. In quiet desperation we search for a solution. We try one suggested path after another; we willingly accept any theory if it promises some small hope. We follow any hero who promises help. But always the same quiet desperation and despair descends upon us as one defeat follows after another. Life is still just one great, unsolvable Gordian Knot.

When will we learn there is but one solution — that to be found in our complete surrender to the young man, Jesus of Nazareth, who in our miracle story proclaims himself to be our champion, the conquering warrior sent from God to overcome the world, even our own little worlds where helpless we lie tangled up within our-selves — our Gordian Knot!

On Calvary's hill 2,000 years ago, in a strange darkness at noon-day, while people jeered and mocked his kingly crown of thorns, our hero took into his blood-stained hands a wooden cross. With the strength of God he swung that cross like a mighty sword and cut cleanly through the knot that binds us all. By that single sever-ing slice of his sword-like cross, he has set us free.

Rejoice, therefore, and be glad, for our Gordian knot-like life has been transformed by a single blow into a new life. We are free from self. We are free for an abundant life in him.

1. Walter Lowrie, *Jesus According to St. Mark* (New York: Longmans, Green and Company, 1929), p. 73.

2. D. E. Nineham, *The Gospel of St. Mark* (New York: The Seabury Press, 1963), p. 75.

3. Lowrie, *op. cit.*, p. 72.

4. *Ibid.*

5. William L. Lane, *The Gospel According to Mark* (Grand Rapids, Michigan: William B. Eerdmans Publishing Company, 1974), p. 72.

6. Sherman E. Johnson, *A Commentary on the Gospel According to St. Mark* (New York: Harper and Brothers Publishers, 1960), p. 47.

7. Edward Schweizer, *The Good News According to Mark* (Atlanta, Georgia: John Knox Press, 1976), p. 50.

8. Barbara Stoops, Religious Editor, *The State*, Impact Section, February 10, 1974, Columbia, South Carolina, p. 1.

9. H. Van der Loos, *The Miracles of Jesus* (Leiden: E. J. Brill, 1968), p. 340.

10. *Ibid.*, p. 241.

11. Alan Richardson, *The Miracle Stories of the Gospels* (London: SCM Press Ltd., 1959), p. 68.

12. *Ibid.*

13. William Barclay, *And He Had Compassion* (Valley Forge: Judson Press, 1975), p. 23.

14. H. Lowe quoted by Van der Loos, *op. cit.*, p. 362.

15. Lane, *op. cit.*, p. 74.

16. William Hendriksen, *Exposition of the Gospel According to Mark*, New Testament Commentary (Grand Rapids, Michigan: Baker Book House, 1975), p. 65.

27

17. Lane, *op. cit.*, p. 74.

18. Van der Loos, *op. cit.*, p. 363.

19. *Ibid.*, p. 366.

20. C. F. D. Moule, *The Gospel According to Mark*, The Cambridge Bible Commentary (London: Cambridge University Press, 1965), p. 18.

Miracle 2

Does Jesus Live Here?

The Healing Of Peter's Mother-In-Law

Matthew 8:14-17; Luke 4:38-41 *(parallel texts)*

Mothers-in-law are much maligned and frequently victimized by cruel characterizations in the jokes of comedians. Not so, however, in Holy Scripture.

In the Old Testament one of the most beautiful stories told is about Ruth and her mother-in-law Naomi. The worst fate that could befall a Hebrew woman happened to Naomi. She lost not only her husband but both of her sons as well. Yet her daughter-in-law Ruth clung to Naomi, and from this relationship we have the most popular words used at weddings to express devoted love between two persons: "For where you go, I will go, where you lodge, I will lodge; your people shall be my people, and your God my God."

Naomi proved to be a good and faithful mother-in-law, for it was her wise advice and careful coaching that enabled Ruth to become the wife of Boaz and eventually the great-grandmother of David, Israel's most illustrious ruler.

The miracle story we now consider is another illustration which shows that all mothers-in-law are not bad. Mark uses it as one of the earliest miracle stories of his Gospel. It is a simple story told in low key without flourishing details. But a breath of homely warmth flows through this brief narrative, and beneath the surface of what is said lies a strong assertion that this mother-in-law was deeply loved by her daughter's husband. Calvin calls this miracle a "home-specimen" of God's divine love and grace.[1]

He Healed Them All

The prelude to our story begins in the synagogue in the town of Capernaum. Jesus was teaching and the people who heard him were amazed. He wasn't like the teachers of the Law; instead he taught with authority. But the people were even more amazed when he healed a man possessed by an evil spirit.

Exhausted by this experience, Jesus left the synagogue and went straight to the home of Simon and Andrew with James and John. They were all looking forward to a leisurely dinner and some quiet moments of much-needed relaxation. But the events which followed show the day had hardly begun for our Lord.

No sooner did he arrive at the home of his friends than he was confronted with a concern demanding his attention: Simon's mother-in-law had taken to her bed with a fever. Despite his exhaustion, Jesus did not hesitate but immediately went to her, took the sick woman by the hand, and lifted her up. She was cured at once, rose from her bed, and gave the men hospitality, a sign that the fever had truly left her.

The news about Jesus — his sensational performance in the synagogue and the instant healing of Peter's mother-in-law — spread like wildfire in the village. People came from everywhere in the region bringing their sick and infirm. Jesus did have the afternoon to himself, because the people waited until sunset when the Sabbath was over and they could safely engage in the labor of carrying their sick without breaking the Sabbath law. That is why Mark says, "When evening came, after the sun had set, people brought to Jesus all the sick and those who had demons." The crowd was so great, and the cases were so numerous, that it was impossible to bring them into the house. So Jesus went out to them. He worked late into the night casting out devils, healing the sick, laying his hands upon them. Without exception he dwelt with each person in need until it could be literally said, "He healed them all."

Three Accounts

Three accounts of this miracle are recorded by the Synoptists. The differences are slight. Mark and Luke place the account immediately after the story of the healing of the man with an evil

30

spirit. In Matthew the healing of Peter's mother-in-law follows the story of the healing of the centurion's servant.

The most obvious difference in the three stories, as Van der Loos points out, is in the various ways Jesus heals the sick lady. Matthew writes, "He touched her hand"; Mark says, "He came and took her by the hand, and lifted her up"; Luke's version is, "He stood over her, and rebuked the fever." Luke's account proves to be the most provocative to scholars, for as Van der Loos says, "It is quite clear that Luke has a demon in mind that had to be driven out."[2] Scholars also speculate as to the exact nature of the disease that sent Peter's mother-in-law to bed. Many assume it was the common cold which could prove very serious in the time of Jesus. Sherman Johnson suggests that malaria was a possibility as this was a common malady in this part of the world.[3] Van der Loos adds a different note to the discussion as he points out that "in the ancient world fever was regarded as an independent disease and not as a symptom accompanying all kinds of diseases."[4]

A Private Miracle
Barclay titles his discussion of the healing of Peter's mother-in-law a "Private Miracle."[5] Herbert Lockyer picks up this thought to ask, "How many homes of the sick and diseased do those modern 'faith healers,' who exploit the suffering for their own financial gain, visit? Home visitation to receive the needy would be too humdrum for them. They require the intense emotion of a large packed hail or tent, with all the paraphernalia of mass psychology to stage their so-called miracles."[6]

Lockyer is perhaps too strong in his reaction to what he calls "faith healing racketeers," for there are undoubtedly faith healers who sincerely feel they are called to serve the Lord in this special way. And one can hardly deny the evidence of many who have been healed or at least helped by these mass meetings for healing. There are also many prayer groups within well-established churches which are effectively enriching their congregation's contribution to comforting the sick within their fellowship.

31

However, the point both Barclay and Lockyer make is significant to our understanding the uniqueness of this miracle story about the healing of Peter's mother-in-law. Here we see Jesus in the privacy of a home and the intimacy of a family environment performing a miracle. The personal and private aspect of this miracle story contributes importantly to its basic message and meaning, as we will see later.

A Bridge

Since this is Mark's first account of Jesus' healing of the sick, Rudolf Schnackenburg believes this little miracle "spans a bridge"[7] to the other miracles Jesus will perform in the remainder of his ministry.

Mark here presents Jesus as not only the one sent to proclaim the coming of the Kingdom but also the healer of the sick and the infirm. Healings are not to be the main concern of his ministry, but Mark desires to establish such acts as signs being given that the demonic which causes man's infirmities is being cast out and overcome by the proclaimer of the Kingdom. In Schnackenburg's opinion, this concept is important, for it shows that the power of Satan is being broken as Jesus begins his ministry in Galilee. Healings, the driving out of demons, are signs that the Kingdom of God has come in Christ.

Perfect Form

Alan Richardson believes that this brief story of the healing of Simon's wife's mother is, in a greatly compressed profile, "the perfect form"[8] of all the miracle stories which are to follow. He sees here the pattern, or outline, of miracle stories in general. (1) The person with a serious need is presented to Jesus. (2) The malady is identified. (3) Jesus acts to cure the afflicted. (4) The cure is announced and there is convincing demonstration that the cure has been fully accomplished. (For example, the fever did not leave Peter's mother-in-law exhausted after she was cured, but she immediately was able to get up and wait upon her guests.) (5) The miracle story "does not merely emphasize the divine power of the Lord; it contains also a moral exhortation: Christians who have been delivered from the power of sin and restored to health should at once begin to use their blessings in the service of the Lord."[9] Richardson concludes from this pattern that there is not a miracle story told about Jesus which cannot be used to instruct us in the Christian faith and give practical suggestions for putting into practice both our faith and the grace we receive from the living Lord.

A Threefold Form

Following the stimulating suggestion of Richardson that this miracle contains a basic pattern or form, let us look at the story by following, not Richardson's exact form, but one helpful for a sermonic treatment of the miracle story. We will consider three central actions that appear in the story.

First: The Request

John Laidlaw in his interpretation of the miracle points out that "the healing was done at the request of those around him."[10] Jesus seldom sought out people in need of healing. This fact does not imply in any way a lack of concern for those in physical need; however, as will be stressed many times in this study of the miracles, Jesus did not conceive his ministry to: be primarily one of working wonders and miraculous healings.

Though Jesus, is often called the "Great Physician" by preachers, he never used or accepted this title for himself. He had come to the sinner and the outcast. He was the "Light," the "Door," the "Way" back to God. He was the "Good Shepherd" who had come to seek and to save the lost sheep. Yet he came not just to heal the injuries they had received falling into the crevice, or to comfort their fears, but to bring them back into the flock of God's own.

In some cases our Lord even avoided healing opportunities, as stated in Luke 4:43, when the people were pushing in upon him to be healed and he said to the disciples, "I must preach the Good News of the Kingdom of God in other towns also, for that is what God sent me to do."

Jesus thought of himself first as the preacher. He had come to proclaim that the Kingdom of God had arrived, the rule of Satan

33

had ended, and Satan's demonic power had been destroyed forever within the world. In our Lord's estimation, redemption was not the saving of that part of man which we frequently refer to as the soul; redemption was for Christ the total restoration of the total person to God. Humans were in a state of rebellion against God, their Father-Creator, separated from him, imprisoned by sin, death, and the devil. Therefore, what was needed was the setting free of God's children and their return to and reconciliation with their father.

When Jesus healed Peter's mother-in-law that day in Capernaum, what he did was an extension of his teaching in the Synagogue. It was a continuation of his proclamation that in him the Kingdom of God had come. He never separated his healing activities from his ministry of the Word.

This means to us that *faith healing* should always be considered as one word. Healing which is from God can never be separated from faith. And since faith is a restored relationship between God and his children, then healing can never be separated into a specialized activity apart from worship, prayer, praise, and thanksgiving. Services that have but one end, purpose, or intent — such as a *healing service* — are actually a denial of the true meaning of "faith healing."

Theodore Parker Ferris was once asked if he believed in faith healings. He answered, "There is no other kind; all healing is faith healing." By this he meant that God works through both pills and prayers to heal people. But note! The emphasis of his statement is not on the word "healing" but on "faith" — faith in God.

In the New Testament, healings were always related to the preaching and teaching of Jesus. No work of wonder, miracle, or sign ever stood by itself; each was always related to the Word proclaimed.

Therefore, since Jesus did not view healings and works of wonder as the primary task of his ministry, the fact that others brought their friends and loved ones to him and requested healing becomes of utmost importance to us. During the ministry of Christ, many undoubtedly came to public gatherings where he was preaching and healing and yet failed to be cured because no one called their great need to our Lord's attention.

This probability says something vital to us as laypersons within the church. How many times a pastor is confronted with the question, "Why didn't you call on Mrs. Jones when she was sick last week?" or "I understand you haven't visited Mr. Smith in the hospital yet." The pastor is hurt by such questions and shaded accusations against his professional integrity. In most cases it is not the pastor's laziness, or neglect, or lack of concern, or even his busy schedule, but the simple fact that no one informed him that Mrs. Jones was sick or that Mr. Smith was in the hospital.

For the pastors I talk with, this omission is one of the greatest frustrations of their ministries. Pastors are not mindreaders; they are just humble servants and they need help to identify those areas and persons where their efforts are needed. As the people in the days of our Lord brought the paralytic, the blind man, the deaf mute to Jesus, so it is our responsibility to inform our pastors and to bring to their attention those who are in need.

When Peter and Andrew told Jesus that the mother-in-law was sick in bed with the fever, this was but the first of a great number of such requests that Jesus dealt with that long, hard, tiring day. Mark states, "When evening came, after the sun had set, people *brought* to Jesus all the sick and those who had demons." Note the word "brought." Then Mark goes on to add, "Jesus healed many who were sick with all kinds of diseases and drove out many demons." Therefore, to the kindly invitation Jesus gives us in the Sermon on the Mount to "Ask, and you shall receive," let us add on the basis of the many miracle accounts in the New Testament, "Ask not only for yourselves, but for others as well." One very important step in this process of bringing others to Jesus is to inform our pastors of others' needs.

Second: The Touch

Walter Lowrie comments that, since this is the first cure of a sick person reported in Mark's Gospel, the fact that Jesus used physical contact "establishes a common means he employed to effect his cures. He touched the one in need."[11]

Nineham is impressed with the fact that "once again the story gives the general impression of a cure performed effortlessly without the need for any magic or special techniques."[12]

Barclay makes this same observation of the effortlessness of Jesus' cure. He comments that many exorcists in the time of Jesus worked with elaborate incantations, formulae, spells, and magical apparatus. But "Jesus heals with a touch and a word."[13]

What does the fact that Jesus healed with the simple touch of his hand mean for us today who stand at a distance of some 2,000 years from the practical possibility of such a touch? Actually the miracle says something very directly to us and to our needs. To understand this meaning we need to focus on the fact that, in referring to this day of healings, Matthew cites the well-known words from Isaiah's great Messianic Passional as fulfilled: "Himself took our infirmities and bare our sickness."

We often hear that by Christ's death he has saved us all and granted us eternal life. But we need also to remember that by his life he assures us he has power to comfort and help us in all our hours of suffering and sickness. The hands that were nailed to a cross to guarantee our everlasting life are the same hands that even now are stretching forth to touch us, to grant us comfort and strength to face the hardships and tragedies constantly challenging and plaguing our daily lives. Christ came not only to free us from eternal death, but to free us from all the destructive miseries of daily life as well.

Sometimes our understanding of the atonement becomes so theologically limited that it means only forgiveness, redemption, justification — words we frequently hear from the pulpit but seldom understand in the pew. We fail to see, as Laidlaw so graphically points out, "The same redeeming energy was shown in these blessed Healings as when in the latest and highest phase of it, He, through the Eternal Spirit, offered Himself without spot unto God."[14] Not only in his death, but in his life, he was in the process of healing us all — totally!

This reality brings the diseases and sufferings of the children of God in every age within the sweep of the healing ministry of Jesus. He "who His own self bare our sins in His own body on the tree," in that same determined deed "took our infirmities, and bare our sicknesses." In the life and death of Christ, passion and compassion become one, and we are touched by the living Lord and

36

receive power to endure whatever afflictions we are forced by circumstances to face.

It should be of great comfort to us all that this little miracle story happened in the home. We are so apt to think of Jesus Christ present in the gathered congregation on Sunday morning, making himself known through Word and Sacrament. And this is most certainly true. But the problem lies in our imagining this to be, as Wallace says, "the peculiar and appropriate setting for Jesus Christ to work in and we are apt to think of him as one who is so absorbed there that he has little time and care to be anywhere else on earth."[15]

However, in the story of this miracle, Jesus is actively present in the midst of ordinary life. He is where we live — in a home. He is where our greatest needs arise in our family relationships and responsibilities. He is where we are.

The miracle of the healing of Peter's mother-in-law shows us that the home is as true and fitting a setting for his work and ministry as any church. Likewise, in a special way, this miracle brings us into touching distance with our Lord, for it takes him out of the ecclesiastical setting and the complex definitions of doctrine and places him firmly at the very center of our daily lives. At every table where people gather together in faith, Christ is present. Even when we dine alone, he is our guest. Beside every bed of sickness and suffering, Christ is standing. In every hour of need, he is our constant companion. Here is our comfort and assurance of the "touching" presence of the living and resurrected Lord.

And it should be added, there is no problem too small for Christ's touching hand of healing. The man in the synagogue had a big problem. He was possessed by an evil demon. Peter's mother-in-law, on the other hand, as many scholars believe, may have had only a bad cold. The miracle story assures us that there is no need so small as to slip through the faithful fingers of God. Therefore, trust God not only with your eternal destiny, but with your daily lives as well. When they nailed the hands of Christ to the cross, by this very act his hands were firmly brought in touch with you and every aspect of your life.

Third: Service

Mark writes, "The fever left her and she began to wait on them." Luke adds the word "immediately." He says, "And immediately she rose and served them."

This is an interesting reaction. She might have rushed out into the streets and shouted for all to hear about the amazing and miraculous powers of this young man named Jesus; or, being a pious woman, she could have gone straight to the synagogue or to the Temple to offer praise and sacrifice to God. At the very least she should have fallen down at the feet of her healer and thanked Jesus with tears of joy and awe. But she didn't. She simply went into the kitchen, picked up some dishes of food, and began to serve her family and Jesus. She did what she had done almost every Sabbath day of her life — she served the Sabbath meal.

A Problem. Some commentators have a problem with this detail of the story because it was not at all customary for women to serve at table, particularly at the Sabbath meal. They did not eat with the men, but were relegated to the place in the house where the food was prepared. Sherman Johnson helps us at this point, for he informs us that "the rabbis generally disapproved of a woman serving at table, but in the villages women have always had more freedom, and the Pharisees still had little influence in Galilee."[16] Since Matthew, Luke, and Mark all agree that this was the reaction of Peter's mother-in-law after she was cured, it would seem that we can accept it as a factual description of what actually happened and move on to what this action means for us today.

Healing Before Service. First, the reaction of Peter's mother-in-law suggests healing is necessary in many situations before a person can serve the Lord.

Some people use sickness as a means of escaping responsibilities. They actually enjoy their illness because it brings attention, and they do not have to exert themselves to undertake tasks which are unpleasant. We have all known this type of person, and it is often difficult to show pastoral patience toward such a person.

This was not the case, however, with Peter's mother-in-law. The fact that she went immediately to work serving her family assures us that her illness was not an excuse but a legitimate reason for being in bed rather than up and at her duties. We find many people in this same situation. They are not only physically ill or handicapped but mentally disturbed, beaten-down, and distressed; therefore, they are in no condition to serve. As a result, all our efforts to challenge them to service are ineffective. They simply do not respond, because they cannot respond.

How many ministers make a call on sick and shut-ins every time they enter their pulpits and preach the Sunday morning sermon! Many of the people before them are sick — sick with troubles and heartaches that close their ears to the words proclaimed. Others are "shut-in-to-themselves" by fears, frustrations, and disappointments. They do not listen to the sermon or respond with active service in the church because they are sick. What they need is to have their "fevers" cured rather than their service challenged.

This need is the reason that a vital part of proclaiming the gospel is pastoral counseling. It is the reason that witnessing to Jesus Christ many times begins with just being friendly with people, willingly listening, and sharing their problems.

Telling the story about Jesus often begins with saying nothing at all about our Lord but listening to the story of the person before you. Letting persons open up and pour out the sickness of their hearts is the first step to witnessing. Before they can believe in and serve the Lord they must be cured, and before they can be cured they must be heard.

Often we hear people say that a word or a kind deed "touched them deeply." What they mean is that the word or deed got through to them where they hurt. That is the kind of "touching" so needed in our interpersonal relationships in the fellowship of faith. These are not the sensational faith healings that dominate conversations when miracles are discussed. But in the long run these are the faith healings which help in building up the Body of Christ, the task Paul so constantly refers to as one of the most important responsibilities within the church.

This simple miracle story about Peter's mother-in-law should therefore constantly remind us to be sensitive to the people around us who first need to be cured — heard and healed before they can rise up and serve the Lord.

Healed For Service. The need for healing leads us naturally into the second message that comes from the reaction of Peter's mother-in-law to her cure. It speaks to us who have already been cured and made whole by the glorious good news of the gospel.

Barclay tells of a great Scottish family which has as its motto "Saved to Serve."[17] That is a motto worthy of being emblazoned on every Christian's heart.

Evangelical Christians who enthusiastically defend the doctrine that we are saved not *by* our good works but by God's good grace so frequently forget that we are, however, saved *for* good works. True, there is nothing we need to do in order *to be saved*, but there is everything we are to do because we *have been saved*. We are set free from sin, death, and the devil, even from the Law, by Christ's vicarious suffering and death upon the cross. However, it needs to be added that we are not only set free *from* something, but also *for* something.

Although we all know this, the miracle story of Peter's mother-in-law provides an additional note to Christian service that is often overlooked. This woman served the Lord in her own way. She did for him what she could do best. She served him his Sabbath meal. As one preacher so aptly put it, "She served him not with her words but with her fingers."

It is the general practice of church leaders to set the standards for Christian service so high that we frighten ordinary people away from serving because they feel they are not qualified. Many do not have the voice to sing in the choir, or the education or knowledge of the Bible to teach a Sunday school class, or the leadership to chair a committee, or the self-confidence to serve on the Every Member Visitation groups.

It is all well and good to assure these people that God doesn't require great talent, only sincere effort; but this only acknowledges and accentuates the inadequacies they feel. For example, a student who wants to help others may feel he is too dumb to become a doctor; so we advise him to become a minister because God doesn't require smart pastors, only sincere ones. That really doesn't help him or the church.

We can serve people and God by being a plumber just as well as by being a preacher. And we can "plow corn" to the glory of God just as much as when we "preach Christ." This is not to degrade plumbers or farmers — or any other profession — over against service callings of ministry or medicine. The point is that we serve God best when we serve him the best way we can, using the talents he has given us. We are all different, yet each person has a valuable contribution he or she can make if only service to the Lord is not limited to some inflexible set of standards for so-called "Christian Service."

We make a joke out of the woman who asked her pastor how she could serve in the congregation, and he said, "Bake a cake for the Thursday night church supper." We may laugh at this and ridicule his mundane suggestion. What's wrong with baking a cake to the glory of God? That may be the very best thing that woman can do for her Lord. And I for one admire and appreciate how much real talent it takes to bake a delicious cake. More power to her! Let's encourage her to bake bigger and better cakes for the Lord. For is that not exactly what Peter's mother-in-law did that Sabbath day at Capernaum? She will be remembered for her service to the Lord long after all the bishops and "Pulpit Princes" of our day are buried in dusty church records and forgotten.

In a large inner-city church, one Sunday morning, the pastor made an impassioned plea for more financial support for their program with the underprivileged of the community. After the service a widow came to him and said that although she had been deeply moved by his sermon there was little she could give. She worked nights scrubbing floors in an office building, and it took every cent she earned to support herself and her children.

But then she added, "I understand you are going to hire another sexton to help in the cleaning of the church. I would like to do that job with no pay. Take the money you would have spent for such an additional worker and use it for your community program."

The pastor could not refuse her. So each morning when she finished her night work in the office building, she would come to the church, clean the rest rooms, dust the pews, and vacuum the carpets. The church was spotless and a pride and joy to the whole congregation.

Years later when this devoted lady was dying, the pastor visited her. He noticed she was disturbed about something. "What's wrong, Mary?" he asked. "Well, pastor," she replied. "I'm about to meet my Lord and he has been so good to me. What can I say to him when he asks what I have done with all the loving grace he has so generously given me?" The pastor was silent for a moment and then he softly spoke. "Say nothing at all to him, Mary; just show him your hands."

Jesus touched Peter's mother-in-law with hands of healing and she was made well. She in turn touched her Lord with hands of service, and he was made glad.

Peter's House

One more approach toward the miracle needs to be considered. Many scholars believe that it is significant that the house of Peter at Capernaum was in reality the first Christian church. Carrington states that Peter's house "became the headquarters of Jesus."[18] Lowrie makes the point that when "Mark mentions the term 'the house' he means the same as if he were to say 'home.' For this house was to be home for Jesus, the only home he was to know from that time on."[19]

Why is this important that a home was the starting place, the cradle, in which the Christian church was born? For one reason, this indicates the personal and family aspects of the Christian faith. Salvation is not something preserved in books. It is not a secret truth written into formal creeds and confessions. It is not the product of a ritual correctly performed in the temple by priests. Rather, it is a spirit-filled life. It is a light glowing within a believer that is seen and felt by all those who come in contact with this one who is possessed with a freedom and a happiness shining forth from a newly-found life.

And where else can such a personal faith find its most natural habitat than in a home — in the warm personal relationship of those who love, and care, and are concerned for one another? Lane says, "The healing accomplished within Peter's home indicates that salvation had come to this house in response to the radical obedience he (Peter) had manifested."[20]

Peter had been caught by the Lord, called and commissioned by him, and undoubtedly Peter's first missionary endeavors were with his own family. We so easily assume that when Peter gave up his fishing business he turned his back on his wife and family, forsook them and ran off, ignoring his responsibilities as husband and father.

Laidlaw points out, this idea is suggested to our minds because of the familiar statement about the disciples "leaving all and following Jesus."[21] Influenced by the medieval monastic picture of renouncing the world and forsaking the natural duties of life, we imagine that Peter deserted his wife and abandoned her to the destitute state of widowhood.

There is, however, nothing in the New Testament to support such a conclusion. We do not know if Peter's wife and family accompanied him; but knowing our Lord's sensitivity to the needs of people, we can, according to Carrington, safely assume that the families of the followers of the Lord were provided for.

Carrington goes so far as to say that "it is probable that the Roman Christians had met Peter's wife; she traveled with Peter, Paul said; and Clement of Alexandria knew a legend that she had suffered martyrdom with her husband in Rome."[22]

The New Testament cannot possibly tell the whole story or spell out each detail of all those who formed the band of followers who accompanied Jesus during those trying three years of his ministry. This miracle story we are now considering, however, gives us an interesting insight into the concern Peter had for his family. It supports the position of those who find it difficult to imagine the disciples forsaking and forgetting their responsibilities for their loved ones as they followed in the ministry of the Lord.

Laidlaw gives strong support to this position when he writes, "These fishermen just as before, kept home and friends and table, and provided as God helped them 'things honest in the sight of all men'; all the more carefully too that they were doing it now, not for their own comfort and support only, but for Jesus and his Gospel."[23]

Peter was a strong and difficult character, an "impediment," as Jesus calls him in Matthew's account, or "satan," as in Mark's; still he was a man with a big heart, impetuous, but with strong emotional ties. True, he was a man who often acted before he thought. He betrayed and denied Jesus in the flickering firelight when he thought the cause he had given his life to had failed; but we must also remember he was the man who captained the church in Jerusalem, and who survived an encounter with Paul in Antioch. And it was Peter who planted the faith with Paul in Corinth and Rome. Certainly we cannot forget that it was he who died a martyr's death for his master and won the homage and admiration of the church at large in a way that Paul, with all his genius, never quite did.

So in many ways this brief miracle is not just another story about Jesus performing a miracle, or even a story primarily concerned with the healing of Peter's mother-in-law, as much as it is about Peter the family man. The account was important enough to be recorded not only by Mark, but by Matthew and Luke as well. Many scholars suggest that the reason was the desire of the early church to stress an important aspect of Peter's personality — namely the fact that he was a devoted family man. This aspect of his character inspired others to accept his leadership in the church and defended him against those who could not forget that he had publicly denied the Lord.

Other interpreters stress the importance of Peter's beginning his missionary activities in his own home, bringing his wife, his mother-in-law, and his whole family to know Jesus. The conversion of families was to become a pattern for evangelism in the early church as it struggled to establish itself in a hostile world. And it was to become the mark of the church — the family of the faithful. This fact reminds us of and reaffirms the truth that faith is best born and nourished within the warm personal relationships of the home atmosphere. How many leaders of the church could testify to the influence of the Christian home on their lives and faith!

Dr. F. Eppling Reinartz, one of the saints of the Lutheran Church in America, often referred in his sermons to "the church in your home." By this he meant that the strength of any church congregation is conceived and tested in the home life of its members.

"Unless religion can be at home in the home," wrote E. Stanley Jones in his book, *The Christ of Every Road*, "no amount of religion in the Temple can save us."

Dr. L. W. Grendstead of Oxford once remarked in his classroom that his favorite story was about the new parson who went to call on his parishioners. He knocked on the door of the first house he came to in the little village. A kind-faced lady opened the door. He introduced himself as the new parson and then asked, "Does Jesus live here?"

"What was that?" came the startled reply.

"Does Jesus live here?" the young minister repeated. After the parson had left, the lady rushed out into the backyard where her husband was tending his roses.

"Frank!" she shouted, "the new parson was just here and he's daft! Just plain loony!"

"What do you mean?" her husband asked.

"Well, all he did was just stand there staring me straight in the eye and repeating again and again the question, 'Does Jesus live here?' I finally had to shut the door in his face."

"Why didn't you answer him and tell him we have always been good reliable members of the church? We attend services every Sabbath and contribute generously to every cause of the Lord's work."

The wife stood for a moment remembering the look in the parson's eyes as he asked the question, and then suddenly it dawned on her what he had really been asking. She turned to her husband, and in the slow, deliberate voice of one who had suddenly seen a vision, she said, "But, Frank, that was *not* what he was asking."

Is this not one of the strong messages that comes through the miracle story we have just considered? Jesus in the home of Simon Peter. Not just an emergency call of a physician to heal a sick member of the family. Not just a visiting preacher coming to a home after church services to pray for an ill member of the household. But Jesus at home in the home of Simon Peter because he was a vital part of their daily lives, a member of the family, one who shared with them their joys, as well as their troubles, encircled

45

their cares with his concern, identified with their suffering and sorrow, as well as their moments of celebration.

Here is the true foundation of the church of Jesus Christ, the home where people love one another and where children are nurtured in an atmostphere of love and concern. It is often said that "families that pray together stay together." But of even more decisive importance is a positive answer to the simple, direct question that ultimately makes of any house a home, "Does Jesus live here?"

---

1. John Laidlaw, *The Miracles of Our Lord* (Grand Rapids, Michigan: Baker Book House, 1956), p. 159.

2. H. Van der Loos, *The Miracles of Jesus* (Leiden: E. J. Brill, 1968), p. 551.

3. Sherman E. Johnson, *A Commentary on the Gospel According to St. Mark* (New York: Harper and Brothers Publishers, 1960), p. 49.

4. Van der Loos, *op. cit.*, p. 553.

5. William Barclay, *The Gospel of Mark* (Philadelphia: The Westminster Press, 1956), p. 28.

6. Herbert Lockyer, *All the Miracles of the Bible* (Grand Rapids, Michigan: Zondervan Publishing House, 1961), p. 171.

7. Rudolf Schnackenburg, *The Gospel According to St. Mark: New Testament for Spiritual Reading* (New York: Herder and Herder, 1971), p. 31.

8. Alan Richardson, *The Miracle Stories of the Gospels* (London: SCM Press Ltd., 1959), p. 76.

9. *Ibid.*

10. Laidlaw, *op. cit.*, p. 158.

11. Walter Lowrie, *Jesus According to St. Mark* (London: Longmans, Green and Company, 1929), p. 80.

12. D. E. Nineham, *The Gospel of St. Mark*, The Pelican Gospel Commentaries (New York: The Seabury Press, 1936), p. 81.

13. Barclay, *op. cit.*, p. 28.

14. Laidlaw, *op. cit.*, p. 162.

15. Ronald Wallace, *The Gospel Miracles* (Grand Rapids, Michigan: William B. Eerdmans Publishing Company, 1960), p. 9.

16. Johnson, *op. cit.*, p. 56.

17. Barclay, *op. cit.*, p. 31.

18. Philip Carrington, *According to Mark* (London: Cambridge Press, 1960), p. 50.

19. Lowrie, *op. cit.*, p. 80.

20. William L. Lane, *The Gospel According to Mark* (Grand Rapids, Michigan: William B. Eerdmans Publishing Company, 1974), p. 78.

21. Laidlaw, *op. cit.*, p. 157.

22. Carrington, *op. cit.*, p. 50.

23. Laidlaw, *ibid.*

Miracle 3

The Man Who Stormed The Kingdom Of God With Violence

The Healing Of The Leper

We hear a great deal today about violence on television, in our streets, and at revolutionary hot-spots around the world. The miracle we now consider is a story Mark tells us about a man who, in his desperation, turned to violence. He was a leper shut off from God, shunned by his fellow humans, condemned to a life of utter loneliness. Between him and the rest of the world was a six-foot chasm of contaminated space across which he could not go. To all who passed by, he was required to cry out the warning, "Unclean! Unclean!"

Then one day something happened to this man. With daring determination, he defied the rules and regulations of the establishment. He broke through the walls of social and religious restrictions and went straight to Jesus. Undoubtedly there was a crowd of people around Jesus that day. When they saw the leper running toward them, they could not believe their eyes. Certainly he would stop before he crossed the forbidden barrier that separated him from clean people. But he didn't. He kept right on coming. Suddenly the crowd scattered in frightened confusion, pushing each other in an attempt to get out of his way. They were horrified, near panic, for even the shadow of a leper falling upon them would be defiling.

At the feet of Jesus, the leper knelt. As Carrington so aptly describes the man's actions, "The leper burst in without apology; he remembers his genuflection but he forgets his manners."[1] His action had been impulsive, reckless, and violent. But now he

49

humbled himself before this man named Jesus and begged for his help. The crowd completely disappeared. The leper was alone, as he had always been. Yet he was not alone, for he was in the presence of a man who was bigger and more powerful than any crowd.

Why this leper rebelled and stormed with violence the walls of imprisonment destiny had placed around him, we can only speculate. It may have been that as a little boy he had heard the Scriptures read in the synagogue telling about Elisha, the man of God, who had cleansed Naaman the leper in the River Jordan. It was his hope that another Elisha would one day come along. It was this daily hope that gave him the courage to endure his humiliating state of existence. Then he heard people talking about a man named Jesus. Some may even have called him the "new Elisha," and the leper felt that his hope had been realized — his one chance had come. So he dared everything — threw caution to the wind and went directly to this man of many hopes.

To Be Like Other Men

This may have been the way it was. But of one thing we can be certain — this leper came to Jesus because he wanted to be like other men. He was a man with a great ambition — not ambition as we usually think of it — being better than others, or getting ahead of others. He simply wanted to be equal with others. His desire was not to pull out ahead of the crowd, but to be a part of it. This is important because how many people do we meet each day with this same simple ambition? They are not the people who stand out in a crowd, but apart from it. We notice them, but for the wrong reasons. They have a handicap or a problem that makes them different. Our reaction is to pity them and make a special effort to help them. But our well-meaning actions are often accompanied by an attitude that is condescending and demeaning. In an attempt to help them, we only increase their hurt. They want to be like other people — treated like other people. They do not want to be singled out, but included.

Not Physical Pain As Much As Mental Anguish

Many times the real pain of a person who suffers comes not from a disease or a handicap, but from the attitudes of those around him. Our thoughtless reactions to other's afflictions separate us from them. It is not intentional and in most cases not even noticed by us, but to the sensitive sufferer we convey in subtle ways our uneasiness and even fear of afflicted people.

In some cases it is a fear of contamination. We fear that we might catch what they have, so we are reluctant to shake hands with them or we avoid touching anything in the room. We stand back as far as we can when talking with them.

Then there is the element of suggestibility. Sick or handicapped people remind us that we, too, are vulnerable to accident and disease. They are a reminder of what might happen to us. We do not want to be around afflicted people because they depress us. We visit them only out of a sense of duty. The afflicted person can sense this and is deeply hurt by it.

In other cases, we are over-solicitous. This is particularly true for the person who is blind, crippled, or suffering from a heart ailment. We destroy their dignity by treating them as if they were helpless. A young man returned from the war with an empty sleeve instead of an arm. His friend, attempting to be comforting, said, "I'm so sorry to hear that your lost your arm." To which the young man immediately came back, "I didn't lose it. I gave it." A middle-aged man returned home from the hospital after suffering a heart attack. After several weeks of being catered to, he finally called his family together and spoke kindly to them, "Look, I am the same person who went to the hospital several weeks ago. My heart attack didn't change me, so please let me live the life God has given back to me as it was before."

So with our leper in this miracle story. He wanted to be like other men, treated like other men. He did not want to be different. He did not want to be singled out; he wanted to be included.

If You Will?

The first words of the leper as he approached Christ were, "If you want to." There is a condition here — a big word, "If." But

51

notice, as Mattheus Keulers points out, "The man doubted Jesus' willingness to heal him, since he was not worthy of healing. He did not doubt Christ's *ability* to heal him."[2] The question of the leper is conditional, but not based on the doubt that Jesus could not heal him; rather, it is based on Christ's willingness to heal him. It is also important that there is no note of demand here. The leper does not come to Christ assuming the mercy of God. He lays no claim on his own right or merit to be healed. He doesn't complain that life has been unfair to him. He gives no reasons why he should be healed. He does not point out how others have it better than he. Nor does he ask the familiar question, "Why did God let this happen to me?" He does not even confess his past sins or his faith and belief in Christ which should have its rewards. He simply looks at Christ and at Christ alone. If there is any hope, it is not in himself but in this man called Jesus.

"If you want to," the leper cries out. It is as if he is saying, "Don't let my faith or lack of it be the decisive factor in my being made clean. Just let your grace and your mercy be the only factor considered." This is the prelude to the gospel. This is where it all begins. This is the attitude that must be present in us if we are to have true faith in God. This is a declaration of dependence that should be the model for us all. "If *you* will!" This places the responsibility for redemption where it should be, not on people but on God alone. The important factor of any faith, if it is to be truly Christian faith, is that it is not what we think or what we do but what God thinks and does. The vital decision is God's decision to choose and help us. The one "giant step for mankind" in the realm of faith is not our step toward God, but his movement toward us. Our belief and love of God is only a response made possible because he first loved and believed in us. The leper cries out, "If *you* will!"

Asking The Impossible

We have pointed out above that when the leper said to Jesus, "If you will," he implied that Jesus can cure him if he only will. This is a tremendous assumption that demands separate attention. William Lane in his work on Mark calls to our attention, "In all the

Old Testament only twice is it recorded that God healed a leper (Numbers 12:10ff; 2 Kings 5:1ff), and the rabbis affirmed that it was as difficult to heal the leper as to raise the dead."[3]

Even as late as the Middle Ages, the disease was considered so final and terminal that when a man became a leper, the priest would put on his stole, take the man into the church, and read the burial service over him. So the leper confronted Jesus with a radical request when he spoke the words, "If you will." And this should assure us that no request is too radical to bring to our Lord. He expects us to ask the impossible, for with him all things are possible.

I Do Want To

Then notice the quick and certain reaction of Christ to the leper's plea. Christ says, "I do want to." What greater words in all of Scripture? God says to desperate people seeking help, "I do want to." This is the gospel. This is the glorious, almost unbelievable good news. God wants — is eager — to help us. Despite our unworthiness, God wants to help us. The whole ministry and message of Christ — his life — his death — his resurrection — are but verses to this one great hallelujah chorus repeated again and again at every great event of his life. God wants to help you.

A little boy and his father, on a hike, came to the top of a high hill where they sat down for a rest. It was a beautiful sight. They could see in all directions the beauties of God's creation. As they sat there, they talked of many things. Then the little boy asked his father, "How big is God's love?" The father thought for a while and then he answered, "Well, if you look to the North as far as you can see, and then to the East, South, and West, looking as hard as you can, God's love is bigger than all that."

The little boy stood up and looked for a long time in every direction. Then he turned to his father. "If that is true, Father, then we must be standing right in the center of God's love." That is where the leper stood and that is where we stand when we are in Christ — right in the center of God's love. And he says to us, "I am willing! I want to help you in any way I can!" That truly is good news — glorious good news. That is the gospel.

53

I Can

Then, if that is not enough, a still more glorious word is added, "I can!" Not only does God want to help us, but he can help us. After Jesus says to the leper, "I do want to," he follows these words with the command, "Be clean!" It is one thing to acknowledge God's willingness. But God gives so much more. He gives us the historic record of his deeds — determined, dared, and done for us. Every event of the Bible is a promise to us that his power is for us — not against us. As Jesus pronounces the leper clean, he promises us that God's love is ours.

Jesus Touches Him

Michelangelo has given us a powerful image of the creative action of God painted into the plaster that covers the ceiling of the Sistine Chapel. He shows us the energetic finger of the Father God stretching forth to touch the limp hand of humanity. It seems that any moment the spark of life will jump the gap between God and people and Adam will be made alive. So in our text God's courageous and creative hand reaches forth to give life. Jesus touches the leper. This was not our Lord's general practice. In most cases he healed with the word only. Gestures and rituals used by most healers of the first century were avoided by Jesus. It was as if he did not want to be identified with the workers of magical cures. But in this case he touched the man. Our Lord did this because he was sensitive to what this particular man really needed. The leper's problem was that he was untouchable. How better could Jesus meet the need for acceptance than with a touch?

Father Joseph Damien went as a missionary to Molokai where lepers were literally abandoned by humanity. They lived in horrible squalor and filth. For sixteen years Father Damien lived among them. He built them a church, provided decent housing with gardens of flowers and vegetables. He brought them a new understanding of what it meant to be human, but somehow he could not get through to them the message of Christ as their Savior. Time after time he would proclaim the message, "Christ suffered and died for you lepers," but with little or no results.

Then one day he was having tea with some of the leaders of the community. Boiling hot water was accidentally spilled on his bare foot and he failed to notice it. His leper friends knew at once that he had developed leprosy because lack of sensation in the extremities of the body is one of the first signs of this dread disease.

Father Damien records in his diary that this was the decisive turning point in his work. For when he next stepped into the pulpit he began his sermon, "My fellow lepers, Christ has died for *us*." From that moment on, the lepers of the island responded and surrendered to Christ as their Savior. Identification with them was the bridge of communication that enabled Father Damien to touch these lepers with the message of the gospel.

So Christ identified with the leper in our miracle story by touching him and by this act the lines of communication were opened.

The Guilty Saved

Wallace is concerned with the element of *guilt* involved with leprosy. "The leper was condemned to his lot by the word and decree of God's priests acting in God's name. And leprosy had come to be regarded as a special sign of God's displeasure."[4] Or as David Redding refers to it, "the dirty sign of God's damnation."[5] Undoubtedly in this day where religion played so vital a role in the daily lives of people, the worst consequence to the leper must have been that he was cut off and separated from God.

Now it is true that lepers could attend the synagogue, but they had to enter before everyone else and be the last to leave. And they were confined while in the synagogue to a little isolated chamber, ten feet high and six feet wide. There is little doubt that lepers must have suffered an unbelievable sense of moral uncleanness. It is therefore easy to understand why many preachers have seen in this miracle story a sign that Jesus can heal our moral uncleanness and sinfulness. As Jesus cured the leper, so he forgives us.

Wallace sees in Jesus' touch of the leper a symbol of how God touches us today with the sacraments of Baptism and the Lord's Supper. Jesus unites himself to us through the sacraments, and by them opens up lines of communication. Wallace writes, "The sacraments tell us that he became flesh of our leprous flesh, in order that we might become flesh of his glorious and perfect heavenly body."[6]

If Christianity seems irrelevant to our needs it may be that we are not allowing Christ to touch us. When we separate ourselves from the church and fail to continually participate in the sacraments, or hear the word, or share in the fellowship of believers, we are pushing ourselves farther and farther away from touching distance with our Lord.

The gospel, however, reveals to us a God who will not take "No!" for an answer. Though we constantly move out of touch with him, he never loses touch with us. On the cross he stretches forth his hands to reach as far as we in our sinful rebellion attempt to run away from him. Therefore, relax and let our Lord touch us — let him embrace us. Then we will know what it means to stand in the very center of God's love.

Justification By Faith

Alan Richardson, approaching this miracle story in the light of the common biblical assumption that disease is evidence of sinfulness, comes to an interesting conclusion. He suggests that, when Jesus stretched forth his hand and touched the leper, he took upon himself the burden of the leper's defilement. Christ became a "sinbearer" for the leper and freed him so that he could now fulfill the law of cleanness. The leper was clean because Christ had taken upon himself both the sin which caused the leprosy and the guilt which resulted from it. What the leper could not do for himself Christ did for him.

Richardson then draws the conclusion, "The whole Pauline doctrine of justification by faith is expounded in this short *pericope*, which carries us to the very heart of the Gospel message of forgiveness."[7] The miracle story thereby becomes a symbolic demonstration of God's forgiveness in action. In the biblical-religious sense, the leper was not just being "healed" — he was "saved."

Nineham also comes to this conclusion as he writes, "The general meaning of the story is to emphasize the surprising nature of salvation now accessible to men."[8] Van der Loos adds, "The

Gospel writers saw this event as a revelation of Jesus' salutary power, as a functon of his Messianic Kingship."[9]

The Leper And The Law

By the act of touching the leper, Christ identified himself with the leper. Actually Christ had to break the same conventions and rules that the leper had broken in coming to him. Christ matched the daring and the violence of the leper. He met him on his own ground of rebellion. Together they defied the law. Not because the law was wrong, but because it was ineffective. Jesus did what the law could not do. The law, as important as it was in the faith of the Jewish people, could not cure or cleanse the leper. The law could do only two things: It could declare the leper clean once he was cured, and it could protect the community from contamination. Nineham writes, "The law could do nothing for the leper; it could only protect the rest of the community against him."[10]

That was all the law could do. Paul recognized this limitation of the law. He saw the law not as redemptive but as regulative. In a sinful world the law could provide order until the power of the gospel could be released, but the law could not cure or make clean. The miracle of the cleansing of the leper serves as a sign that in Christ something new was happening. It illustrates the surprising nature of our salvation that is now accessible to us in Jesus the Christ. Jesus was setting us free from the law not by the destruction of the law but by creating new persons. The law was not changed — the law remained the same — but humanity had been changed and made clean and new. So we are free from the law not because Christ did away with the law; rather we are free from the law because Christ makes us new persons. As a butterfly is transformed from a worm groveling in the dirt, so we are lifted from the confining rut of the law and given a new form of existence. The old earthly habitation is still beneath us, but we are free to rise above it in the new world of the spirit. On the surface it may appear that, by touching the leper, Jesus is breaking the law, but in reality he is breaking *through* the law to create a new way of life for us.

In the annals of Switzerland, Arnold van Winkelried is honored in song and story as Switzerland's most famous hero. At the Battle of Sempach the Swiss army faced the Austrian knights. The Austrians stood as a solid wall of flesh and steel against the Swiss. Again and again the Swiss attempted to break through the Austrian ranks, but to no avail. Finally Winkelried cried out to his companions, "Follow me. I'll make a bridge for you to victory." He threw himself upon the spears of the enemy, gathered as many of them as he could into his arms, buried their points in his own body, and, pulling the knights forward and downward, fell himself, pierced through and through. But his massive body formed a human bridge through the Austrian ranks and the Swiss army literally marched across the body of their fallen hero to certain victory.

So the law stood before us a barrier — an impossible barrier that we could not get over, around, or under. Then Christ came and placed his body upon a cross, took the guilt of our sins into his own body, and thus formed a bridge through the law that we might enter into the Kingdom as clean and renewed children of God.

Jesus Sends The Leper Back

Our Lord's relationship to the law is further clarified as we see him sending the leper back to the very institution which both he and the leper had defied. But he sends the leper back a new man. It is as if our Lord is saying to him, "Go to the priest and discover for yourself what I have done for you. You are clean. You are a new man. Now the law will not condemn you but only affirm that you are clean before all people."

So with us. In Christ we do not fear the law. We rejoice in it as the will of God. For it is no longer a series of demands that we *must* do, but an obedient way of living that we *can* do because we are new persons in Jesus Christ.

Snort Of An Impatient Horse?

At this point in our miracle story, there is a sticky phrase that scholars are not quite sure how to handle. Mark says, "Then Jesus spoke *harshly* with him and sent him away at once"(v. 43). The verb could be translated "sternly warned" or "charge." Hendriksen,

58

with many other scholars, points out that the verb comes "from the idea of the snorting of an impatient horse, or simply in general from the idea of making a noise in anger."[11] The problem is that the story begins with Christ showing compassion on the leper, then suddenly the note of anger is struck.

Lowrie expresses the majority opinion that Jesus is not here speaking to the leper but to the leper's condition, or more to the point, to "the evil one who had revealed itself in the horrible affliction of the man." Or as Lowrie expresses it, "At the monstrous tragedy of human life, at the hideous evil that can reduce a man to such a plight."[12]

A young prince sheltered all his life from the real world one day saw a decrepit old man, a dead body, and a putrefying corpse. That was enough to affect the conversion of Gautama Buddah and begin a religion that was to conquer most of Asia. Certainly, then, it should not be surprising to see our Lord repelled by suffering and strike out against the evil which causes it.

The important homiletical value of this section of the miracle story is, as Schweitzer says, "Pity is not the reason for the healing. The reason is to be found in a far more comprehensive campaign which is waged against every ungodly thing and in which the special authority of Jesus is revealed."[13] Jesus believed that in his healing miracles he was engaged in a proper conflict with sin, death, and the Devil. Christ should not be pictured here romantically as the great physician with his little black bag filled with miraculous remedies for all ills; rather, it is necessary that we see him as the wrathful warrior challenging the forces of evil that hold his people captive. Compassion? Yes, a compassion not of simple pity but a burning compassion that issues forth in an aggressive anger against the evil one.

Incriminating Evidence

Another phrase which causes problems is the little phrase "a testimony to them." Does "them" refer to the people or to the priests? If it means the people, then it could be a simple statement that the people should again admit the leper back into the community. Or it could mean that Jesus was demonstrating to the people that he does not disregard the law.

If "them" refers to the priests, then Jesus could have wanted the priests to "see that he had not come to break the laws and regulations"[14] or it could mean our Lord's desire to reveal to the priests that he was truly the Messiah whose work it was to heal lepers.

Van der Loos holds to the interpretation that this statement of Jesus is spoken in testimony against the priests. It is "incriminating evidence against them." What Jesus meant was, "It will be damning evidence against the priests if they establish that a healing has taken place and accept the cleansing sacrifice but do not recognize the person and power of the healer."[15] And does it not follow that many are condemned who accept a miracle and fail to acknowledge the healer? In all the miracle stories, the greatest miracle is Christ himself. The basic issue is rarely the factuality of the miracle event, but the Christology of the one who witnesses or hears the miracle story. The acid test is not the question, "Do you believe in miracles?" but, "What do you think of Christ?" If you truly believe that Christ is the Son of God, then miracles should not come as a surprise or as a problem, but as the natural, expected consequences of the personhood of Christ. As Theodore Parker Ferris has said, "Unusual people do unusual things."

Christ Is Hindered, Not Helped

The text ends on a note of irony. Jesus instructs the leper to tell no one about what had happened to him that day, but to go directly to the priest. However, the leper was so excited about his newly-found life that he could not contain himself. He rushed forth and told everyone he met what this man Jesus had done for him. And Mark says, "He talked so much that Jesus could not show himself publicly in the town." The irony of the situation is that the position of the healer and the healed are exchanged. As the leper was once an outcast isolated from society, now Jesus becomes an outcast unable to show himself before people. The leper undoubtedly thought that he was doing the right thing. After all, Jesus had done a great and marvelous work and he wanted to tell others about it. But he was doing what *he* thought was right and not what

Christ had instructed him to do. The results were harmful to the cause of Christ. Lane reminds us, "This incident serves to terminate the preaching tour of the Galilean villages."[16] How true it is that our Lord continues to suffer because of our foolish and reckless actions.

No Easy Thing

So our study of this miracle began on a note of violent disobedience that was right and ended on a note of violent disobedience that was wrong. A man defied convention and religious restrictions and violently broke into the presence of Jesus seeking to be made clean. That was the right thing to do, for Jesus healed him and made a new man of him. But then the leper violated the advice of Christ to be silent about his cure, and the results were harmful rather than helpful to the cause of Christ. That was the wrong thing to do. So our miracle story shows that encountering Christ and following him is not easy. There are moments that call for courage and daring. There are other moments that call for caution and obedience. Christ takes a whip and drives the moneychangers from the temple, but he also takes a towel, and gets down on his knees and washes the disciples' feet. The important thing, therefore, about following Christ is to realize at the beginning that there is no simple pattern or consistent style of life that we are to mechanically or legalistically follow to the letter. Rather, the important thing is that we are to live in Christ close to his Word and sacraments and remain keenly sensitive to the daily directives of his Holy Spirit. Faith is an exciting adventure. Sometimes we are challenged to daring and violent actions. At other times we are called to cautious actions and obedience. Sometimes we are to take the whip and stand up to all corners; at other times we are to take the towel and kneel down to everyone. But of one thing we can be certain — following Christ will never be dull.

---

1. Philip Carrington, *According to Mark* (London: Cambridge University Press, 1960), p. 54.

2. Keulers quoted in Van der Loos, *The Miracles of Jesus* (Leiden: E. J. Brill, 1968), p. 483.

3. William L. Lane, *The Gospel According to Mark* (Grand Rapids, Michigan: William B. Eerdmans Publishing Company, 1974), p. 89.

4. Ronald S. Wallace, *The Gospel Miracles* (Grand Rapids, Michigan: William B. Eerdmans Publishing Company, 1960), p. 16.

5. David Redding, *The Miracles of Christ* (Westwood, New Jersey: Fleming H. Revell Co., 1974), p. 75.

6. Wallace, *op., cit.*, p. 19.

7. Alan Richardson, *The Miracle Stories of the Gospels* (London: SCM Press Ltd., 1959), p. 61.

8. D. E. Nineham, *The Gospel of St. Mark*, The Pelican Gospel Commentaries (New York: The Seabury Press, 1936), p. 86.

9. Van der Loos, *op. cit.*, p. 494.

10. Nineham, *op. cit.*, p. 86.

11. William Hendriksen, *Expositon of the Gospel According to Mark,* New Testament Commentary (Grand Rapids, Michigan: Baker Book House, 1975), p. 80.

12. Walter Lowrie, *Jesus According to St. Mark* (London: Longmans, Green and Company), p. 91.

13. Edward Schweizer, *The Good News According to Mark* (Richmond, Virginia: John Knox Press, 1970), p. 58.

14. Van der Loos, *op. cit.*, p. 487.

15. Van der Loos, *op. cit.*, p. 89.

16. Lane, *op. cit.*, p. 89.

Miracle 4

The Miracle Of Forgiveness

The Healing Of The Paralytic

Luke 5:17-26; Matthew 9:1-8 *(parallel texts)*

This miracle story is unique, because it tells of an event which interrupted a sermon. And an unusual interruption it was. Jesus had been preaching about the Kingdom of God when suddenly pieces of dried clay and bits of brushwood started to tumble down from the ceiling. The startled congregation took their attention from the preacher and watched with stunned curiosity as a hole was formed in the ceiling by fingers clawing away at the mud structure. And then, to the open-mouthed amazement of the crowd, through the yawning gap in the roof the body of a man lying on a mat was lowered to the floor in front of Jesus.

There was a stunned silence. No one spoke. No requests or pleas for help were spoken — just the silence broken only by the sound of the last remaining bits of debris as they broke loose, fell, and hit the hard floor. Then Jesus spoke, "My Son, God is not angry at you."

This is a strange story, filled with suspense, surprise, and spiritual depths. For here we see our Lord revealing a side of his personality seldom seen. He invades the prerogative of God and speaks a word of pardon and power. He does what even the Messiah cannot do. He forgives sins. And to the surprise of all, the earth does not open up and swallow him. Is it any wonder that Mark ends the story by having the people say, "We've never seen anything like this before"?

The Characters Of The Drama

The plot begins when four men who have heard about the healings of Jesus decide to take their paralytic friend to him. It took time to get the stretcher ready and prepare the paralytic for the trip, so they were late in arriving at the meeting. By the time they got there, the crowd was so great that the stretcher-bearers could not get close enough to the master to present their friend. But such an obstacle is only a challenge to men of determination and ingenuity. Where they could not find a way, they made one. They climbed the stairs to the flat roof of the house and with their bare hands tore an opening in the ceiling and lowered their helpless friend to the feet of Jesus. But it was worth all the risk and effort, for their friend, who before could look at life only from the flat of his back, now stood tall like other men. He was given new legs and because of this he was now able to look at life with new eyes.

These persons involved in this drama have been suggestive to interpreters of distinct types of behavior we find in the Christian Church.

Roadblockers

The first and largest group are the roadblockers. This was the crowd whose presence at the door of the house prevented the paralytic from entering to see Jesus. Some take on the role of roadblockers quite deliberately. They view the church as the gathering of the good. They assume the responsibility of sentinels guarding the church from the contamination of undesirables. They set up their own standards for being a member of the fellowship. They keep away those who do not measure up to "our" church. They refuse to speak to strangers and fail to make them feel welcome, particularly those who look different and come from a social status or ethnic background different from their own. Oh, they are polite with their exclusiveness, suggesting that such people would find a "better" church home "down the street" where they would be more happy with their "own kind."

Most roadblockers in the church, however, are not this intentional; they simply get in the way without even realizing it. They are so engrossed in straining to see Jesus themselves or struggling for a front row position so that Jesus won't miss seeing them, that they fail to see they are standing in the way of those outside who need to be brought into his presence. They are so hung up on assuring their own personal salvation and assurance of heaven that they overlook the lonely, the brokenhearted, the frightened, and the insecure. Their favorite hymn is "Jesus Savior, Pilot Me," and the heck with everybody else.

Then there are those roadblockers who represent their faith poorly. They claim allegiance to Christ and boast of their perfect attendance record and generous stewardship, but display in their daily contacts with others greed, prejudice, and hypocrisy. They misrepresent their Lord to the world and thereby stand as roadblocks to people searching for a meaningful life of faith.

Stretcher-Bearers

The second type found in our story are the stretcher-bearers, represented by the four men who bring their friend to Jesus. They live their lives opened to the needs of others, are willing to sacrifice themselves, give their time, go out of their way to help others come to Christ. They are not overaggressive salesmen forcing or harassing people to buy into Christendom; rather, they are quiet and personal in their approach showing genuine interest and concern for people. They are always ready and willing to give a helping hand to anyone who indicates an interest in knowing Jesus Christ. They witness to God's love in their own sincere love for others.

For the most part, these are unnamed people. They form the supporting cast without which the play could not go on.

When Linus discovered he was only going to be the innkeeper in the Christmas play with no lines to speak, he refused. But Lucy assured him, "True, you didn't get a lead part, but without you there will be no Christmas pageant." So this army of unnamed men and women marches across the pages of Scripture. They never see their names up in "lights," but the light which is Christ could never be seen without their quiet unapplauded support. Stretcher-bearers — those who carry others to Christ and then quietly slip away into the background of the history of salvation. We need more of them!

65

Barrier-Breakers

The third type are the barrier-breakers. These are the aggressive leaders within the church who are represented by the action of determination that tore the opening in the roof above our Lord. They are the people who, finding some ways blocked, make new ways to Christ. In times of stress, God calls, empowers, and directs these people to stand up and meet the challenge of their day. When Israel was in slavery, God raised up a Moses to lead the chosen people to the promised land. When the children of God turned from God to follow their own ways, God empowered an Isaiah, a Jeremiah, an Elijah to prophesy and call the people to turn about-face. When the Gentile world needed to be invaded, a Paul was directed to lead God's people across forbidden frontiers. When philosophy was about to supplant theology, an Aquinas and an Augustine were called. When ritual and church structure were about to smother the gospel, God raised up a Calvin and a Luther to free people with the knowledge of the true and lively Word. In our own day, when the Roman church became immune to the course of human history, God raised up a John XXIII who brought the warm blood of common humanity back into the anemic arteries of the church.

This is always our hope. In every hour of darkness and despair and religious depression, God raises up, calls, and empowers barrier-breakers who open up new ways — where no new ways are found, they make them.

So these types of persons — the roadblockers, the stretcher-bearers, the barrier-breakers — form the background of our drama. They create the setting in which our Lord might act and reveal himself to us.

The Faith Of Friends

Mark then directs our attention to Jesus. "When they had made an opening, they let the man down, lying on his mat." Then Mark adds, "When Jesus saw *their* faith." Scholars are concerned with who the word "their" refers to. Does Mark mean the faith of the four men who brought the paralytic to Jesus, or does the word "their" include the paralytic?

Van der Loos believes this statement to be an important issue, as all the Gospel writers who record this story are unanimous that Jesus paid heed to this expression of faith. He is convinced the word "their" included the faith of the sick man. He writes, "There is no reason to assume that 'their faith' must be confined to that of the bearers; they all believe in the power of Jesus,"[1] by this he includes the faith of the paralytic. Many interpreters disagree.

Sherman Johnson in his commentary on Mark takes the most reasonable position when he states, "Here the man's own faith is not excluded, but that of his helpers is emphasized."[2] When the faith of the friends is taken as important, we are confronted with the issue of "representative faith," a vital aspect of the New Testament's understanding of faith.

Representative Faith

The concept of representative faith is often difficult for us to understand, as we view faith as an individual possession of a particular person. It is one of the virtues of human personality like courage, honesty, and a sense of humor. And to some extent this is true. But faith is so much more. It is a shared virtue of a fellowship. It is something we possess because we are a part of something bigger than ourselves.

To understand faith we need to see that the idea of individuality, as we use the word, is foreign to the biblical mind. The Bible does not think in terms of an individual but of a person, and there is a vital difference. To discover an individual you isolate a person, insofar as possible, from all outside influences and relationships. It is the sterile laboratory approach of the scientist who attempts to isolate the specimen to be studied into as vacuum-like an environment as possible so that the object can be known in and of itself.

However, a person in the biblical sense is established by just the opposite approach. Here you are concerned to see the person in his environment and to discover all the inter-personal relationships possible. You are concerned to know what kind of a husband he is to his wife, what kind of a father to his children, what kind of a son to his parents, what kind of a neighbor to the people who live next door. Personhood is discovered and realized in relationships.

The Bible is concerned with people, not as individuals but as persons. God calls and establishes "a people" — "persons in a relationship." He does not deal singly with them but corporately. When Christ comes to establish the Kingdom, the first act of his ministry is to establish a discipleship — a family where faith might be a corporate experience shared in a fellowship.

It is true that no one can have faith for another, but it is equally true that no one can have faith without another. The faith we possess has been given to us by God through others. Faith does not fall miraculously from heaven like manna. It is not discovered dormant deep within ourselves, awakened with our own self-determined effort. No! It was given to us by God through our parents, teachers, pastors, or friends who witnessed to us and told us about God our Lord and Savior.

There is the well-known story about a man visiting hell. People were seated about a table loaded with luscious food, but every one of them was starving to death. The reason was obvious — every person's elbow was bound with splints so that it was impossible for the people to bend their arms and bring the food to their mouths. The same man visited heaven. The situation was surprisingly the same — a table loaded with food. People seated before it with their elbows bound, but there was one decisive difference — everyone was well fed.

The visitor turned to his guide. "Why," he asked, "are the people in heaven well fed when they wear the same elbow-binding splints as those in hell?" "Well, my friend," the guide replied, "here in heaven the people have discovered that even though they cannot bend their elbows to feed themselves, they can with unbending arms feed each other."

So faith is a shared experience in fellowship. We cannot possess faith for another, but we can enable another to have faith. At that strange banquet described above, no one could *eat* the food for his neighbor. Each person had to do his own eating, but no person could eat without being *fed* by another. So faith is corporate. Faith depends on a fellowship where we share faith with each other, thereby enabling all to have faith.

During a hike in the woods, some young people came across an abandoned section of railroad track. Several of them tried walking the rails, but eventually lost their balance and tumbled off.

Two little boys, off to the side watching the attempts, were laughing and whispering. Then they jumped onto the tracks. They offered to bet anyone that they could both walk the entire length of the track without falling off. Challenged to make good their boast, the two boys standing on opposite rails joined hands, thus balancing each other, and proceeded to walk the entire section of the track with no difficulty whatever.

So as we attempt to walk alone through life in faith, we so easily lose our balance and fall. What we need is to join hands with others in faith and then we can achieve the delicate balance needed to maintain faith.

Our miracle story of Christ healing the paralytic is dramatic enactment of the inter-relatedness which is the faith situation. Someone told someone who told someone who told the four men about Jesus Christ. And they carried the precious cargo of their helpless friend to the feet of Jesus. It was in a stranger's house and not his own that he was healed. It was a complex cluster of circumstances that made possible the miracle story. So many hands had helped that one man's legs might be healed and his heart made whole.

The Gesture Of Faith
In addition to the word "their" in this statement made about Jesus, there is another provocative word, "saw." "When Jesus *saw* their faith." Lourie points out that this reminds us that "faith is a thing that can be seen."[3]

So often we think of faith in terms of inner belief, or the confession of a creed, a commitment made, or a story testified to. But faith is also something to do. It can be seen in a person's face. A truly holy faith is expressed in a happy face. How seldom do we Christians look like redeemed people and how seldom do we act like it.

When we stand at the check-out of the supermarket do we treat the cashier as a part of the register, automatically scanning the items, or is she a person to us? Do we consider that they have stood longer serving a line than we have waiting in it? Do we realize they pay the same outlandish prices for food that we do? Do we treat them as persons with feelings and needs just as we have? Are we kind, considerate, and caring? A smile, a friendly word, acknowledging them as persons — respecting the dignity of their humanity — are gestures of faith that can be *given* and seen!

A few months after moving to a small town, a woman complained to a neighbor about the poor service at the local drugstore. She hoped the neighbor would repeat her complaint to the owner.

The next time she went to the drugstore, the druggist greeted her with a big smile, told her how happy he was to see her again, and if there was anything he could do for her just to let him know.

Later the woman reported the miraculous change to her friend. "I suppose you told the owner how poor I thought the service was?" she asked.

"Well, no," her neighbor answered. "In fact, I told him you were amazed at the way he had built up this small town drugstore, and that you thought it was one of the best managed drugstores you'd ever seen."

Now this neighbor was not only wise in the ways of this world; she applied her faith in the positive power of love. She treated that druggist as a person for whom Christ had died. We do not have to ask everyone we meet if they have been saved to witness to Jesus Christ and his gospel. We can do it with our friendly, considerate attitude, our actions of kindness and courtesy, and our practice of love. Faith is something that can be *seen*! Mark writes, "When Jesus *saw* what faith they had."

God Is Not Angry With You

The first word Christ speaks to the paralytic is, "My son, your sins are forgiven." This can be best understood if we express what Jesus is saying in more familiar terms. Namely, Jesus is saying, "Son, God is not angry with you."

This handicapped man was a Jew and he had been taught all his life that suffering was a direct punishment for sins. If a person were ill, it was because he had displeased God. Misfortune, affliction, and pain were all ways in which God punished the offender against his holy will.

Today many of us feel the same way. Although we no longer believe there is a direct relationship between suffering and sin as the Jews did in Jesus' day, deep down inside ourselves we have a feeling that when something goes wrong in our lives we have done something bad. One of the ways some parents punish their children is to send them to bed without their supper. Similarly a person lying on a bed of pain feels he is being punished. They ask, "Why did this happen to me?" or "What did I ever do to deserve this?"

There is little doubt that we have all done sufficient wrongs in our lives that no matter what suffering we have to face, it is deserved. But this was not the teaching of our Lord, nor is it the theological position of the Christian faith today. Afflictions are caused by the natural process of cause and effect, in a fallen world where there is suffering, disease, and death. Because we live in this fallen world we are the victims of it. Now in one sense we are responsible, for as persons we share the inheritance of a race that has rebelled against God and brought the world to its fallen state. But individual afflictions are not the direct result of personal sins.

The paralytic, however, being a man of his day, believed he was standing under the judgment of an angry God. He came to Jesus knowing he had done wrong and was being punished for it. The first thing Jesus does is to set the record straight. He says, "God is not angry with you." Or in other words, "This crippled condition of your body is not God's doing. It is not his will; rather God wants to help and heal you."

This is the starting point of any problem facing us — the knowledge that God is not angry with us but wants to help and heal us. As we strive for healing, wholeness, and happiness, God is on our side! God is not working *against* us but *for* us!

Change Needed

Since the Jews as a religious race accepted affliction as divine punishment for their sins, they felt that the first thing that had to be done was to change God's attitude toward them. God was angry and therefore needed to be appeased. So they created a complex

71

system of offerings and sacrifices designed to change God. Christ came with the message that it was not God who needed to be changed but us. God loves us and wants us to be whole, but we refuse his offer of love.

A little boy visited his grandfather who was seriously ill with a contagious disease. He watched his grandmother boil in scalding water all the dishes that his grandfather had used. After several days of seeing his grandmother going to all this trouble, he remarked to her, "Wouldn't it be easier to boil grandfather?"

Behind this childlike remark is a profound truth. It would not only be easier but more efficient and that is the position taken by the New Testament theology. What is needed is not to purify our environment but to purify us. It is not the circumstances of the world about us, but the state or condition within us, that holds the solution to our problems. Christ came with the teaching and the proclamation that we must be born again — that is that *we* need to be changed — not God. We need to be washed and cleansed not with boiling water, but with the water of the spirit that in our baptism makes us new men and women.

A young bride from the East followed her husband to an Army camp on the edge of the desert in California. Living conditions were primitive, at best. The only housing they could find was a run-down shack near an Indian village. The heat was unbearable in the daytime — 115 degrees in the shade. The wind blew constantly, spreading dust and sand over everything. The days were long and boring.

When her husband was ordered farther into the desert for two months of maneuvers, loneliness and the wretched condition got the best of her. She wrote to her mother that she was coming home — she couldn't take it any more. In a short time she received a reply. The letter contained just two lines:

Two men looked out from prison bars.
One man saw mud, the other stars.

She read the lines over and over again, each time feeling a little more ashamed of herself. She knew her husband loved her and she didn't want to let him down. All right, she'd look for the stars.

In the following days, she set out to make friends with her Indian neighbors. She asked them to teach her weaving and pottery. She began to study the desert. She learned the forms of the cacti, the yuccas, and the Joshua trees. She collected seashells that had been left millions of years ago when the sands had been the ocean floor. She became an expert on this area and began to write a book about it. She was happier than she had ever been in her life. What had changed? The heat? The desert? No! She had changed.

As baptized Christians, we have been changed and cleansed. We no longer stand under God's judgment and condemnation, but within his love. The tragedy is that we still live in the mud and fail to see the stars. We do not realize and utilize the great gifts of faith and grace which God has so freely given to us.

God does not force forgiveness upon us. He respects our freedom. He sends his son to die for us. He establishes the good news of this forgiveness in the Holy Scriptures and even provides the Holy Spirit, enabling us to appropriate that forgiveness in our lives. But he will go no further. We can still refuse it, ignore it, live as if it were not so. And that is why it is so important that we hear the Word constantly promising our forgiven state. The beginning step to the solution of all our problems is the knowledge — the awareness — the appropriation — the celebration of this first fact of faith: "My son, God is not angry with you."

Reactions Varied
The reactions to these words of Jesus to the paralytic first were varied. The people there that day expected to witness a healing, but Jesus pronounced a word of absolution. Some were surprised, others were disappointed, and a few were angered.

Surprise
Most of the people in the crowd were surprised. Some were even shocked to find a man in the streets forgiving sins — even a man who claimed to come from God. For, in the times of our Lord, forgiveness was not the common experience of worship that it is today.

Forgiveness was an extremely limited experience. Forgiveness was associated with the temple and particularly with the Day of Atonement when one man, the High Priest, penetrated the forbidden veil of the temple and stepped into the Holy of Holies where God dwelled. As the representative of the people, the High Priest stood in the presence of God awaiting his word of forgiveness. The people stood outside in wonderment and awe, separated from the Holy God by a massive system of ritual and regulations. Forgiveness was a dim and distant thing — something that was handed down to them indirectly from the priests.

Then suddenly and unexpectedly a carpenter's son stands in the streets and speaks the words — the words of God himself. "My son, your sins are forgiven!" Is it any wonder that most of the people were surprised and some even shocked? Forgiveness pronounced by a layman in the streets rather than by the High Priest in the courts of the temple? Luke expresses this when he states the reaction of the crowd at the end of his account of the story. Literally, he has the people saying, "You would never believe what we saw happen today!"

Disappointment

As some were surprised and shocked, others were disappointed. They knew that Jesus had been preaching and proclaiming across the land that the Kingdom of God had come. That is why they were there that day. In their minds the Kingdom meant, "No more want! No more tyranny! No more disease!" This is what they wanted to hear. After all, it was the promise of their beloved prophet Isaiah:

> *Then shall the eyes of the blind be opened and the ears*
> *of the deaf unstopped;*
> *then shall the lame man leap like a hart and the tongue*
> *of the dumb sing for joy.* — Isaiah 35:5-6

They were an earthly people and to them the Kingdom meant health, wealth, security, and happiness, for all. As they stood there watching the exciting scene of the paralytic lowered into the presence of Jesus, they expected to see a miracle — the material dreams and visions of their old prophets of Israel actualized before their eyes. The lame man would, any minute, leap up like a young deer. A work of wonder! A miracle right before their eyes! How exciting! But instead Jesus simply and softly spoke to him, "My son, your sins are forgiven."

The crowd was disappointed, but none so much as the four men who after great trouble had finally managed to bring their paralyzed friend into the healing presence of Jesus. They were not concerned with forgiveness and guilt; their ritualistic systems and priesthood took care of such matters. They were practical men. They were concerned with healed legs, not liturgical pronouncements of forgiveness.

Now we can identify with and understand their reaction, for how often we have felt the same way, faced the same disappointment. Our God is a God of love and power; therefore, why doesn't he do something directly about our urgent human problems — poverty, disease, bad housing, starvation, social justice, and human rights? We, too, are an earthly people. We have to live every day with suffering and slums all about us. Why doesn't God work a few of his miracles today — for us? What is so frustrating is that we try hard and fail; but for God it would be such an easy, effortless task. Just a minute movement of his finger and all the headaches and heartaches of our world would be cured.

Jesus, however, gives no encouragement to our desires for quick and easy solutions. In fact, he deliberately directs our attention in the other direction. He does not deny our dreams for physical and material perfection; he just puts them in the proper order of priorities.

When he is faced with the Canaanite woman and the issue of Jew and Gentile and their places in the Kingdom, he follows a carefully conceived order. First, the Jews then the Gentiles. So here he places material, physical problems in their right place in God's order of things. And as we see from the miracle story before us, they are not in first place.

Christ says that the first thing to be dealt with is the basic relationship between God and his people. This means that forgiveness is first. Then — when we are restored to a right relationship to our

God — then, as Wallace points out, "He will fulfill the further promise of complete healing of the redemption of the bodies of men from corruption and death, and the bringing in of lasting human happiness and prosperity."[4]

We need to remind ourselves that when we are called to proclaim the coming of the Kingdom, that coming is expressed in the signs of people being released from the burden of guilt, the removal of the fear of judgment and the restored relationships with God and our fellowmen. We are not called to promise the immediate release of suffering and sickness, want and war, disease and death. These issues which plague all of us must be endured with patience and hope, knowing that in their proper order and in God's own time, these things, too, shall pass away and physical wholeness and earthly peace will be ours. Until then we are to trust God.

Anger And Delight

The first reaction of the scribes was one of anger. They were men well schooled in the written Law of God and its oral interpretation. According to Lane,[5] also considered themselves guardians of the teaching office. There was little doubt in their minds of a direct relationship between sin and suffering. All disease and physical handicaps were the direct result of sin. If a person were to be cured, he must first be forgiven. So they believed and so they taught.

The scribes, however, were not in Capernaum by accident this particular day. They were intent upon gathering evidence against Jesus in order to build up a case against him that would eventually hold up in court. They listened carefully to the sermon Jesus preached. Apparently there was nothing he said that disturbed them. Then the sermon was suddenly interrupted by the appearance of the paralytic. Again, nothing too disturbing. It was what they had expected, having heard of Jesus' reputation as a healer. But then Jesus broke the awkward silence created by the interruption of his sermon and spoke the words, "My son, your sins are forgiven!" The scribes were instantly angered, but afterwards when they had a chance to compose themselves, they were smugly delighted.

Their instant anger was for two reasons. First, as Harvey points out, Jesus did not speak "with the voice of a prophet (who might have claimed to know that the man was about to recover, and who could have said in virtue of this knowledge, that it must be the case that the Lord had forgiven him). Jesus declared outright that the man was forgiven and so implicitly claimed the authority to dispense God's forgiveness himself."[6] This was sheer blasphemy to the scribes. No man could forgive sins — only God could. This young upstart from Nazareth is not just claiming to be a prophet sent from God; he is assuming to be God.

And if this were not enough, he is also misrepresenting God. The Lord of the Temple ritual would never speak so casually about forgiveness. The very structure of their religion demanded that forgiveness be taken seriously. In the estimation of the scribes, Jesus was taking forgiveness too lightly. And this was the second reason for their instant anger.

Sherman Johnson summarizes the belief of the scribes: "Forgiveness depends, according to Judaism, on true repentance — sorrow for sins, open acknowledgment of it, and resolute turning away from it, together with such restrictions as may be possible."[7]

The scribes heard no word of repentance from the paralytic, no promise to live a better life. They heard no words of penance from Jesus, no reprimand — no restrictions — no instructions to lead the better life and obey the Law. Is it any wonder that in the scribes' estimation Jesus was not only guilty of assuming a role exclusively belonging to God, but he was also robbing forgiveness of its meaning?

Cheap Grace

Today we would identify this objection of the scribes as being the complaint of cheap grace — the idea that God forgives without the requirement of repentance. Whenever the gospel of free and unmerited forgiveness is proclaimed, there are always those voices who raise the objection, "Cheap grace!" And this is natural, for people are incurably self-oriented. If the forgiven person pays no price personally, then grace is cheap. But grace given by our Lord can never be called cheap, for it cost him his very life to freely give it.

When Jesus claimed the right to freely pronounce the paralytic forgiven, he did it seeing the shadow of the cross falling across his path, and he knew that he had come to offer himself a ransom for our forgiveness.

During the American Revolution, a father took his young son to a hill above a valley where American patriots had just driven back the British forces at great cost. Spread before them was a vast valley of suffering and death. The smoke of battle still lingered in the air. The snow-covered ground was dyed red with patriot's blood. The moans of wounded and dying men softly broke the deadly silence. The father placed his arm about his son and, looking toward the valley below, said, "Look long and well and remember — this is the horrible cost of your freedom!"

Who dares stand before the hill of Calvary and face the cross whereon our Savior dies? Who can view those innocent hands and feet pierced by cold nails of iron — that side torn open by a soldier's spear — that holy head crowned with thorns — who can look into those lonely, longing, loving eyes of our Lord hanging there for us with mocking spittle running down his face, mixed with tears and blood, and declare any act of God's grace "cheap"?

We may cheapen ourselves by failing to appreciate and appropriate the grace of God into our lives, but in the light of the cross, no grace which comes from God is cheap. For the passion and pain of that cross is the price Christ pays for our forgiveness. Therefore, look long and well and remember.

The Tables Are Turned

As we have pointed out, the immediate reaction of the scribes was anger; but, when they had pulled themselves together and remembered why they had come to Capernaum, they were delighted. They had come desiring proof and they now had it. Jesus was definitely guilty of blasphemy. There was no doubt about that. He, a mere man, had forgiven the paralytic's sins and only God had the power and the authority to do that. Positive proof! That's what they came to get and that's what they had.

But, cunning men that they were, they kept their mouths closed. This was not the right time to publicly accuse Jesus and declare him a blasphemer. They were determined to destroy him and they knew this required the right time and the right place to expose him.

Jesus, however, proved still more cunning than they. He read the crafty minds of his enemies. He exposed their hidden secret thoughts, and directly confronted them: "Why are you thinking such wicked, vicious thoughts?" The scribes were taken aback and truly shaken. Their cover had been suddenly blown. Jesus continued, "Which is easier — to tell this man his sins are forgiven or to tell him to get up and walk?" What a question! Neither is easy. Both forgiveness and healing require divine power. And in the same breath Jesus added, "But that you may know the Son of Man has power on earth to forgive sins." Then he turned to the paralytic and said, "Rise, take up your bed and walk." And the healed man left for home with his bed-roll tucked neatly under his arm.

Great! With a single, simple stroke, Jesus crushed the insinuation that his forgiving the paralytic was a mere pretense. The scribes wanted incontrovertible proof that Jesus was a blasphemer. Jesus turned the tables on them. He mounted a marvelous counterattack and gave them incontrovertible evidence that he was God! What a Lord!

A Validating Sign

Now the words Jesus spoke to the scribes create some problems for the interpreters. Here Jesus says, "I will *prove* to you that the Son of Man has authority on earth to forgive sins." Many times before, Jewish leaders had challenged him to present a sign that would prove his claims and each time he had refused. But now, without being asked, he gives a sign to, in his own words, *prove* his act of forgiveness.

It may have been that in the past Jesus refused to do signs because he was being tempted by the Jews. Now he did it by his own decision — not directed by anyone except God. But there is another possible explanation. What Jesus is doing here in this miracle is not so much *proving* his authority as *validating* it. The difference is slight but significant. To prove something, you provide evidence to produce a change in attitude on the part of an accuser or to influence an opinion. To validate something, you support it with an additional claim. You literally bind the action, stamp it with approval. To validate you enhance the action rather than argue its truth with evidence.

This is what Jesus is doing, validating his action of forgiveness with the additional action of healing. If Jesus could read their minds and recognize their thoughts, then he also knew that no proof would change the scribes' minds. And he was right, for even though it seems that Mark includes the scribes when he describes the reaction to the miracle with the words, "They were all amazed and praised God," we know the scribes were not convinced or amazed. They were angered and perhaps a little disappointed that their scheming silence had backfired on them, but above all they were determined — deadly determined — to destroy Jesus. That very night they met together and passionately plotted how this blasphemer might be publicly exposed and eliminated forever.

The Son Of Man

The second term which concerns interpreters is Jesus' use of the title "Son of Man." It appears in the New Testament some eighty times and always on the lips of Jesus. It was the favorite title he used to refer to himself.

Jones remarks that it is "a semi-poetic Aramaic expression which in itself means simply 'man.' "[8] In Daniel 7:13-14, the Son of Man was a person of authority, sovereignty, glory, and kingly power. He was a real hero figure, a man of the people, a superstar who would restore the Jewish people to an ascendancy among the people of the world that was being denied the Jews at the present time. As Harvey points out, "In the days of our Lord the 'Son of Man' figure fired the imagination of the Jews."[9]

Geldenhuys is convinced that here Jesus is directly presenting himself as a Messianic figure. "His Messianic claim could not have been more uncompromisingly made; and it is plain that for him the title 'Son of Man' was primarily one which denoted his Messianic dignity — one moreoever, which he habitually preferred to 'Messiah' because of the political connotations which the latter bore in the popular mind of his day."[10] Most scholars disagree and feel that this is just too early in his ministry for such a public presentation of his Messiahship.

So far as our study is concerned, it is enough simply to see Jesus here claiming the right and the authority to forgive sins on earth. His use of the Son of Man title is but another example of the way in which he claimed authority without a direct reference to himself. His question to the scribes is not, "Do you think I have the authority on earth to forgive sins?" but, "I will prove to you that the Son of Man has authority on earth to forgive sins." It is left to the listener to make the connection between Christ and the Son of Man.

The Miracle Of Forgiveness

Luther, who always stands with his feet firmly planted upon the earth when he speaks of heavenly things, strikes directly to the practical application of this miracle story. Focusing in on the phrase "on earth," he begins his sermon on this text with the words, "This Gospel teaches us to note particularly the good tidings which God has granted to us, that we may here on earth say to each other 'Thy sins are forgiven thee.' "[11]

Luther finds God giving the right to each Christian to pronounce the forgiveness of sins to his neighbor. In the same light, Fridricksen believes this miracle story was used by the early church to validate its right to forgive sins — a right given to Christians by Christ himself. He writes that here the early church is giving "assurance of the forgiveness of sins to each repenting sinner, referring this power back to Jesus himself."[12]

The power to forgive which Jesus exhibits here he later gives to his followers. In Matthew 18:18, Jesus says, "And whatsoever ye shall loose on earth shall be loosed in heaven;" in John, our Lord states, "If you forgive men's sins, then they are forgiven; if you do not forgive them, they are not forgiven" (20:23).

Luther states that this means, "God puts the words of forgiveness into the mouth of men." And he adds, "Though you hear but the voice of men you nevertheless hear God and receive forgiveness of sins."[13] This is a fantastic assumption and so it was first received.

81

Scholars in Luther's day objected to this and claimed that by this statement Luther was making gods out of men. Luther's response was that men do not possess the power in and of themselves to forgive sins, as Christ did, but we have the Word which possesses the power to forgive and we have been given the authority to pronounce that Word — to speak that Word and thereby assure another person that God has forgiven him.

The position of Luther and the contemporary opinion of Fridricksen is that this miracle story is concerned primarily with the miracle of forgiveness. Fridricksen writes, "The issue here is of a man for whom forgiveness is the real miracle, whereas the healing is secondary."[14] Wallace agrees, "Everything else that happened that day was secondary, and simply illustrated and complemented what this first great miracle of forgiveness had accomplished."[15]

Today we frequently take forgiveness for granted. Failing to take seriously the problem of guilt, we overlook the tremendous power we have been given by God to exercise the right of absolution and forgiveness. Though we seldom acknowledge it, guilt underlies most of our failures to accept ourselves and relate to others. What is needed is the insight of our miracle story, which reminds us that we cannot love and forgive until we first know that we are loved and forgiven by God. We need to share with one another the miracle of forgiveness, for it can still work miracles in our life and in the lives of others.

A nurse had lost her faith after she came to the big city. One night she was working in the hospital when the ambulance brought in a young woman who had been stabbed in a drunken brawl in a disreputable quarter of the city. Her case was helpless and the nurse was asked to simply sit by the unconscious girl until death came.

As the nurse looked down on the coarse lines of this girl's hardened features, the girl's eyes slowly opened and she spoke, "I want you to tell me something and tell me straight. Do you think God cares about people like me? Do you think he could forgive anyone as bad as me?"

The nurse hesitated for a moment. Her first reaction was to run away. But something held her there and she answered, "I'm telling you straight: God cares about you and he forgives you." The girl slipped back into unconsciousness. A few days later the nurse went to her pastor that she hadn't seen in more than ten years, and she told him this story and then she added, "You know, something happened to me that night. I felt that somehow it was I who was being forgiven."

People today may not know they need forgiveness, for they tend to speak of their basic needs as being accepted and wanted. They desperately cry out in the silence of their own inner being, "Does anyone care? Does anyone care whether I live or die?" Like the dying girl in the hospital and the nurse who sat beside her, their question is, "Do you think God cares about people like me?" Our responsibility is to translate that need to be "cared for" into its biblical equivalent, which is forgiveness. The world desperately needs to hear the word of divine absolution, "My son, my daughter, God is not angry with you."

Horton and Tittle[16] support the idea that this miracle story suggests that forgiveness is not only delegated by God to the official clergy of the church, but to every individual Christian. But they then add a much-needed note. They both point out that it is not only with words but also by our actions that we pronounce absolution. When we receive wrongdoers into our fellowship and accept people as they are in love, we are declaring God's forgiveness.

It should be remembered that when Jesus was reproached for his inclination to forgive sinners, the evidence his accusers presented was, "This man receives sinners and eats with them." So in our treatment of unclean, undesirable people — the people so frequently rejected and condemned by society — we testify and witness to the forgiving love of God or we deny it.

As Luther stressed, the Word is still primary in forgiveness and there can be no power to our forgiveness apart from the Word, but deed and action are also needed to confirm the Word. First Jesus spoke the Word, "Son, your sins are forgiven." Then he performed the deed: "Take up your bed and walk." Both together form the miracle. For us today the basic issue is not the relationship between sin and suffering but between word and deed. The miracle of forgiveness demands both!

Steimle speaks to this when, in a sermon on this text, he begins by answering the question Jesus asked, "Of course it's easier to say 'your sins are forgiven,' than to say 'arise and walk.' After all, every Sunday in our worship services we declare sin forgiven. But in how many churches is the paralytic given strength to rise and walk Sunday after Sunday?"[17]

Steimle goes on to point out that Christ is first concerned with the "hopeless emptiness in the man's eyes, rather than to his obvious physical distress of not being able to walk."[18]

The conclusion Steimle comes to is that little is gained if a man's paralysis is healed and he has sound legs to walk on but has no reason to walk. What is needed is a purpose and a reason to walk. And somewhere worthwhile to walk to. This comes through forgiveness which in its simplest terms means acceptance. This acceptance means "to get up and go about whatever business you have with new zest, with confidence, and purpose and joy — a new creation."[19] Then we are no longer a part of the problem but a part of God's creative and redemptive answer to the needs of our time.

Forgiveness is the true miracle in the healing story of the paralytic and today it is still the most amazing miracle God performs in the lives of people. And, wonder of wonders, God invites us to share in it — to proclaim to our friends and neighbors, "God is not angry with you." Let us all join hands and walk in faith together!

1. H. Van der Loos, *The Miracles of Jesus* (Leiden: E. J. Brill, 1968), p. 443.

2. Sherman Johnson, *A Commentary on the Gospel According to St. Mark* (New York: Harper and Brothers Publishers, 1960), p. 56.

3. Walter Lowrie, *Jesus According to St. Mark* (New York: Longmans, Green and Company, 1929), p. 97.

4. Ronald S. Wallace, *The Gospel Miracles* (Grand Rapids, Michigan: William B. Eerdmans Publishing Company, 1960), p. 26.

5. William L. Lane, *The Gospel According to Mark* (Grand Rapids, Michigan: William B. Eerdmans Publishing Company, 1974), p. 95.

6. A. E. Harvey, *The New English Bible Companion to the New Testament* (London: Cambridge University Press, 1971), p. 119.

7. Sherman Johnson, *op. cit.*, p. 56.

8. Alexander Jones, *The Gospel According to St. Mark* (New York: Sheed and Ward, 1963), p. 77.

9. Harvey, *op. cit.*, p. 120.

10. Norval Geldenhuys, *Commentary on the Gospel of Luke* (Grand Rapids, Michigan: William B. Eerdmans Publishing Company, 1951), p. 353.

11. Martin Luther, *Sermons on the Gospels*, Vol. II (Rock Island, Illinois: Augustana Book Concern, 1871), p. 503.

12. Anton Fridricksen, *The Problem of Miracle in Primitive Christianity* (Minneapolis: Augsburg, 1972), p. 131.

13. Luther, *op. cit.*, p. 513.

14. Fridricksen, *op. cit.*, p. 133.

15. Wallace, *op. cit.*, p. 30.

16. Walter Marshall Horton, *Our Eternal Contemporary* (New York: Harper, 1942), pp. 82-84. Ernest Fremont Tittle, *The Gospel According to Luke* (New York: Harper, 1951), p. 51.

17. Edmund A. Steimle, *Are You Looking for God?* (Philadelphia: Muhlenberg, 1957), p. 31.

18. *Ibid.*, p. 31.

19. *Ibid.*, p. 38.

Miracle 5

There Are Demons In The Sea

"The Stilling Of The Storm"

The Sea of Galilee is as dangerous as it is beautiful. Located 680 feet below sea level, it has a fertile climate that is almost tropical. The hills surrounding the lake are carved deep with ravines and gorges which act like gigantic funnels drawing the cold winds toward the sea. In a matter of seconds, the calm surface of the water can become a raging, churning cauldron.

Such was the experience of the disciples in our story. The day had been a busy one. Mark states that Jesus had preached his message to the people using many parables. The people had listened attentively but few understood. Jesus was exhausted, so he left the crowd, took his disciples with him, and got into a boat.

Barclay points out that, "The boats of the Galilean fishermen were quite large and a little unwieldy, with one mast and one great triangular sail. At the stern of the boat, just in front of the helmsman, there was a little platform-like deck and on it a cushion, and it was the custom that distinguished guests sat there while the boat sailed."[1]

Apparently Jesus went to the back of the boat, stretched out on the pillow and went to sleep. Suddenly a strong wind blew up and the waves were so large they began to spill over into the boat. The disciples panicked and rushed to wake the sleeping Jesus. "Teacher, don't you care that we are about to die?" they cried out. Jesus got up, and commanded the winds and the waves to be still. The winds died down and there was a great calm. Jesus, however, was not so calm; he turned to the disciples and said, "Why are you

87

so frightened? Are you still without faith?" But the disciples could not answer him. They were so amazed at the sudden calm of the sea that they could only say to each other, "Who is this man? Even the wind and the waves obey him!"

This is the way Mark tells the story. Matthew and Luke tell the same story, except that they all have a slightly different version of the exact words Christ spoke to the disciples. Matthew (8:26) has Jesus saying, "How little faith you have." Luke (8:25) states that Jesus asked them, "Where is your faith?"

Allegorical Interpretation

There have been several approaches taken by interpreters to this little miracle.

The historical approach has been that of allegory. Each detail of the story becomes a representative symbol. The boat is the church; the sea, the life situation on which the church sails. The storms are the troubles and the persecutions that the church encounters.

Luther saw this miracle as a parable of life. When Christ enters our lives we should expect that storms and tempest will follow. Luther also saw the story as a lesson teaching us "the nature of true faith, how it braves the battle and the storms and comes to Christ relying upon his help."[2]

Van der Loos is very much to the point when he speaks against such allegorizations of this miracle. He writes, "But when the fishing boat which was once in distress on the Sea of Galilee is converted into the 'ship of the Church,' it should be realized that this conversion is affected purely and simply in the shipyard of the imagination."[3]

Topical Interpretation

A common homiletical use of this miracle is to withdraw from the story a topic such as "fear," or "faith," or "the Word" and proceed to develop a sermon not on the total text but simply the selected topic. For example, Chapel has a sermon based upon this miracle entitled "Defeating Our Fears," where he develops the general theme, "Faith Overcomes Fears."[4]

Spiritual Interpretation

Close to the allegorical approach is the popular interpretation which spiritualizes the storm and sees the miracle as an example story that Jesus can and does bring peace to us in the midst of any of the storms that life thrusts upon us. William Barclay, for example, in his book *And He Had Compassion*, identifies the various storms of life — the storms of temptation, passion, worry, and fear. He concludes that "if we remember that Jesus is always with us, we will find the storms of life become a calm."[5]

The Focal Point Of The Miracle

There are two possibilities when looking at this story. The one places the focus on the disciples and their faith or lack of it. The other places the focus on Jesus and his power over nature. They are related and could possibly be combined into one sermon, but for the sake of clarity let's look at each separately.

Desperate Disciples

When the disciples and their problem is our main concern, then the story becomes an account of human faith, or lack of it.

The "what" of the story becomes the fear of the disciples in the midst of a storm. According to Wallace, the faith of the disciples failed. The storm had entered and so captivated their minds that their faith was driven out. The implication that the disciples had *no* faith, or what little faith they had was destroyed is a possible interpretation based on the accounts of Mark and Luke where Jesus asks, "Where is your faith?" or "Are you still without faith?" But it would cause some problems with Matthew's account where Jesus says, "How little faith you have."

Wallace points out that the cry to Jesus for help was motivated by the fear of the storm rather than faith in Jesus.[6] Now it is true that fear is destructive. There is the classic legend of the peasant who gave an old lady a ride. When he discovered that her name was Cholera, the dreaded plague, he made her promise him she would kill no more than ten people in his village. When she left the village, one hundred people had perished from the plague. The angry peasant took the knife she had given him as a pledge of her

89

promise and started out after her. When he finally caught up with her on the road, she grabbed his hand that was raised to kill her and assured him she had kept her word. "I killed only ten," she said. "Fear killed all the rest."

President Roosevelt, in his first inaugural address (1933) during the terrible depression, said to the nation, "The only thing we have to fear is fear itself."

It is true that much of the social reform that we see about us is motivated by fear rather than faith. Much of the equal rights movement was motivated by the public fear of racial riots and political upheavals. It was not so much a victory of faith in human dignity as fear of inhuman reprisal.

And this is wrong. For not only did Jesus come that we might be motivated by faith, but that fear might be overcome. He constantly called us to resist fear with faith. He said to the disciples, "Let not your hearts be troubled, neither let them be afraid" (John 14:27). And John adds (1 John 4:18) that fear is to be cast out by "perfect love."[7] As we are commanded to love, we are equally directed not to fear. The disciples, therefore, had failed. Fear had overcome them. But it does not necessarily follow that they had lost all faith. Matthew presents Jesus as seeing in the situation "little faith." This seems to be more consistent to the plot of the story. For if the disciples had lost all faith, it would seem that their actions would have been far more radical. The first reaction to terror is foolish panic. When the cabbage leaf fell on Chicken Little and she thought that the whole sky was tumbling in, her panic foolishly drove her straight into the den of the dreaded fox. So the disciples, gripped by sheer terror, would likely have done something foolish and irrational, like jumping into the sea. But they did not; they went to Jesus.

The other common human reaction in a state of total fear is to be scared stiff, to be paralyzed and able to do nothing. But the disciples did not freeze in their moment of terror. They turned to Jesus. And this would seem to indicate that they did have enough faith to turn to their Lord.

Little Faith

Here, as in many other passages, the issue is not the amount of faith but the quality of faith. Faith as a state or relationship to God is extremely complex, because it involves the total facilities of a person — what he thinks, what he feels, what he does.

Rodin created his great statue, *The Thinker*, to represent thinking as action — positive, painful action. He wrote, "What makes my thinker think is that he thinks not only with his brain, with his knitted brow, his distended nostrils and compressed lips, but with every muscle of his arms, back and legs, with his clenched fists and gripping toes." So with faith; the total person is involved. The problem with the disciples' faith in the fishing boat is that it was only emotional. They were in danger and Christ was asleep. If only they had stopped to think about their situation, they would have reasoned that the presence of Christ awake or asleep was sufficient security for their salvation. Christ wasn't apart from them; he was with them. But they didn't stop to think. They simply reacted emotionally. When Jesus criticized their faith, he was not referring to the amount or quantity of their faith. They had a great amount of faith in him when they cried out, "Save us!" But it was all emotional. Jesus pointed out to them that their faith was too narrow, too limited; it should have included their minds — their thoughts — their thinking.

Often this is true of our faith. It is simply emotional. When God is bombarding us with evidences of his presence, we have no problem believing. As long as we can feel God at work in us, our faith is strong. But when God is silent, when he seems to be asleep and unaware of us, our faith leaves us.

A little boy was taking a train ride for the first time. When it came time to go to bed, his mother put him in the upper berth and told him not to be afraid because she was there, his daddy was there, and God was there and they would all look after him. When the lights were turned down, the little boy called out, "Mother, are you still here?" "Yes, dear." "Is Daddy still here?" "Yes, dear." "Is God still here?" "Yes, dear." About five minutes later the voice was heard again, "Mother?" "Yes, dear." "Are you still here?" "Yes, dear." "Is Daddy still here?" "Yes, dear." "Is God still here?" Five minutes later the same thing and on through the night until about one o'clock, the little voice was heard again. "Mother?" "Yes, dear." "Are you still here?" Then a great, gruff voice at the end of the pullman rumbled through the car, "Yes, your mother's here. Your daddy's here. Now shut up and go to sleep." There was a sudden silence in the train, and then the little voice spoke up once more, "Mother, was that God?"

So with us. When our faith needs voices, visions, and feeling to sustain it, our faith is immature — little faith. It needs to grow up, to mature to the point that it involves our minds, our thoughts, and attitudes as well. We need to reach the point that we know God is present even when we cannot feel him or sense his presence. This happens when we stay close to his Word, study it, and make its message a part of our total being.

We need to add, however, the lack of a mature faith which the disciples exhibited did not mean they were lost. They may have lost faith in Jesus, but he had not lost faith in them.

It is to their credit that, faced with a storm and the resulting fear, the disciples took what little faith they had and placed it in Jesus. Because of this the situation did not overcome them, but it was the presence of Christ that made the difference.

Luther catches this point in his sermon when he comments that the little faith the disciples possessed was enough in the presence of Jesus. Great faith doesn't need Christ's assurance or presence. Great faith stands before God without need of the support and strength of a savior. Little faith needs a Christ! Luther writes, "If the faith of the disciples had been strong ... they would have said to the sea and the waves: Beat against us as you may, your forces are not strong enough to overthrow our boat, for Christ our Lord is on board with us...."[8] The disciples had only a little faith but they invested it in a big *Lord* and that is why they were not destroyed.

The Object Of Faith

The important aspect of faith is not the amount we have, but the object of our faith. A little faith *in* Christ is sufficient, for it is Christ and not the quantity of our faith that eliminates fears and calms storms.

There were two men; one had $50,000 to invest and the other had $5,000. The man with the $50,000 invested his money in a fly-by-night business that ultimately failed. The man with $5,000 invested it in a solid, reliable growing business. Today the man who had $50,000 is broke, but the man who had $5,000 is now financially secure.

So with the disciples; they took what little faith they had and placed it in Jesus. When even a little faith is entrusted to a great Lord amazing things are bound to happen. A mustard seed can move mountains, and the miracles are marvelous to behold. For the decisive issue is not the amount of faith but the object of our faith. And there is no greater than Christ our Lord to place faith in.

A Healthy Fear

So far in our discussion we have assumed that all fear is bad and should be overcome. Let us pause for a moment and consider this miracle from another point of view — healthy fear.

When William Barclay deals with this miracle, he titles the chapter "The End of Worry and Fear." He takes the position, as we have pointed out above, that many scholars, teachers, and preachers have when dealing with this miracle, namely, faith overcomes fears, and that is good. Barclay comes to the conclusion that we can pray away our terrors, if we have enough faith. His last statement is, "If we remember that Jesus is always with us, we will find the storms of life become calm."[9]

It is true that we cannot deny what difference the presence of Christ makes in a person's life, nor do we deny the power of prayer. However, when we look at the story of this particular text, there are some problems with such an interpretation. During the storm the disciples are afraid. They turn to Jesus and he calms the storm — but he does *not* calm them. Mark and Luke state and Matthew implies the disciples were far from calm. Mark states at the end of the account, "They were *terribly* afraid." So far as the story is concerned, the fear of the disciples is not calmed or eliminated but transferred from fear of the storm to fear of the person of Christ himself. They cry out in fear, "Who is this man? Even the wind and the waves obey him!" In the light of this, the point the miracle

93

story makes is not *how* to overcome fear, but of *whom* we are to be afraid — the demons in the sea or the Lord over the sea? And the answer is obvious — we are to fear the Lord.

Now this is not to deny that Jesus wants us to overcome our fears and not be afraid. But faith overcoming fear should not become an overall general principle that is applied to every situation. There are times when fear is good. There are times when fear is an ally of faith and not its enemy. The Old Testament, particularly the Psalms, are filled with positive views of fear: "Serve the Lord with fear" (Psalm 2:11). "In thy fear will I worship" (Psalm 5:7). "I will teach you the fear of the Lord" (Psalm 34:11). "The fear of the Lord is the beginning of wisdom" (Proverbs 9:10). This fear means, of course, not the panic that filled the disciples in their little storm-tossed fishing boat; it means instead a healthy respect for the power of God. But both fears, the fear the disciples exhibited toward the storm and the fear we should have toward God, come from a common basic view of life that we are not in control. There are powers far greater than ourselves that ultimately determine the outcome of our lives.

This is the meaning of this miracle story — not how faith overcomes fear, but in whom we should put our faith *and* our fears. Who is it that ultimately has control of our destiny? Is it the demons that dwell in nature, or is it the Lord Christ? This is the real issue of this story — not how much faith *we* have, but how much *power God* has over our lives. This places the focal point of the story not on the disciples and their faith, but upon Christ and his power.

The Cosmic Christ

When we place the focus of our attention on Jesus, then he becomes the important *who* of the story which determines the plot of this miracle. And it becomes a story about the cosmic dimensions of Christ and his power and authority over all of nature.

A fierce storm is stilled. The Greek word used here is often translated "*rebuked* the winds and the waves," which literally means *be muzzled* or *gagged*. The suggestion is that the storm is a demon that is to be bound and gagged.

There Are Demons In The Sea

The disciples were men of their age. They shared the world view of their time. It was a simple understanding of the world in which they lived. Every kind of trouble, disorder, and disaster was due to demonic forces. These forces were personal — they were creature-like servants of the evil one. Therefore, the actions of nature were not an unbreakable chain of cause and effect; nature was governed by powers which possessed personalities and wills. Disease, deformity, and mental disturbances were signs of demonic possession. Storms, earthquakes, and all disasters in nature were the raging activity of demons. History was a battlefield where the forces of good struggled to survive against the forces of evil.

When the storm suddenly arises from nowhere, the wind beats against their faces, the lightning strikes, and the waves whip like a mad monster about them, threatening to capsize their little boat, the disciples must have thought that a whole legion of demons had attacked them. Their cry is a cry of cosmic terror, "Save us, Lord, we are perishing." This was not just the cry of men fearing a storm and death; this was a scream of sheer fright in the presence of the demonic. They were not just afraid of dying; they were afraid of falling into the hands of the evil one.

Not Man's Faith But God's Power

Jesus awakes from his sleep. He stands up and, Matthew records, "... gave a command to the winds and to the waves and there was a great calm." The fact that Jesus spoke not to the disciples but to the storm would also suggest that the issue here is not man's faith or lack or it, but God's power.

If the intent of the miracle had been faith and man's need of it, then it would seem that Christ would have spoken a word to the disciples. He would have issued a commanding word with one of two results. Either he would have given a word of faith to the disciples so that they might destroy their fears, or he would have given them a word that would have enabled them to have faith despite their fears. The meaning of the miracle would then certainly be an example of how faith overcomes fear. However, Jesus speaks not to the disciples, but to the wind and the waves.

The reaction of the disciples supports this, for they were amazed not that they had been given faith, but that Christ had authority and power over the demonic in nature. "Even the wind and the waves obey him."

Jesus did not pray to God asking him to still the storm, which is what the disciples more than likely expected in such a situation. Rather, to the disciples' surprise, Jesus acted like God and spoke like God. He spoke a word of authority and power — the demons fled — the winds retreated — the waters responded and were calm. All the forces of nature, good and bad, obeyed the Lord. Because of this, the disciples came to realize that their ultimate destiny was not decided by the demonic but by God. And in some mysterious way this man Jesus was God exercising his power and authority here on this earth.

Demons Today?

Now what does this say to us today? We no longer believe that demons are at play in our world causing disease and disaster. Or do we? Are there not evidences that we still believe in impersonal forces which have power in some way to determine our destiny? We call these forces fate, luck, chance. We talk about odds and averages. We read our horoscopes and follow the science of astrology.

We laugh at the ideas of demons but we knock on wood for luck. We practice all kinds of strange superstitions. We construct our offices, buildings, and apartment houses with no thirteenth floor. When things go wrong we remark, "What will be will be." When we lose, we say that fate was against us. We spontaneously wish each other, "Good luck."

It seems that no matter how sophisticated we become, we hold on to the belief that there are basic forces which operate willfully within our world and somehow determine our destiny. To this common attitude our miracle says — our lives are not determined by chance, fate or luck, but our lives are in the hands of God. And he and he alone will determine our ultimate destiny.

The Gripping Hand Of God

God determines our destiny and this is our hope, our joy, for the God we are to fear because of his great power is pure love. God is love and held in his grip of grace all fear is cast out. Fear brings us to recognize the power of our God, thus enabling us to experience the full effect of his love for us. God's love is not the weak affection of the romantic; rather it is the gripping, strong, and courageous love of the redeemer.

A brilliant young Hungarian named Gabriel came to Oxford to study the philosophy of science. But all the while he was studying, his mind kept returning to his homeland now under the harsh heel of Communist occupation. Finally, he knew what he must do.

He returned and gave himself to the struggle for freedom in which his people were secretly engaged, working as a leader in the underground resistance corps of Christian youth fighting to free their beloved country from the pagan Russian yoke. After little more than a year, he was arrested, brought to trial, accused of treason, found guilty, and sentenced to death. The night before he was to die, his brother who was an influential member of the local Communist party, came to him in his prison cell to make a proposition. "Denounce publicly Jesus Christ," his brother said. "Let us use your statement as propaganda for our country's youth and we can guarantee your safe passage out of the country and back to Oxford."

Without hesitation, Gabriel calmly but firmly refused. "But why?" pleaded his brother. "Why throw your life away for something so uncertain as faith? You are a sensible, intelligent, scientifically-trained young man. Can you prove all these things you confess? Can you prove the virgin birth, the incarnation, the resurrection? Can you prove that Christ even lived?"

"No," answered Gabriel.

"Then why?" argued his brother.

Gabriel was silent for a moment. Then, reaching into his torn and dirty shirt, he brought out into the dim light of the prison cell the little gold communion cross that hung from a chain about his neck.

"Why?" Gabriel answered, studying thoughtfully the simple cross that lay in the palm of his hand. "Because, before I heard the message of this cross I was lost and alone and afraid, just like you are. But once I heard the words of my Lord from the cross, once I learned from these God's great desire to love me for his own, from that moment on I was no longer lost, no longer alone, no longer afraid."

The next day they took Gabriel out into the drab, gray yard of that prison and stood him against the wall. In the cold, crisp morning air the rifles cracked and his strong young body crumpled to the snow-covered ground. He died still clinging to that simple little cross in his hand.

I know this because, several years later, after the bloody Hungarian revolt, Gabriel's brother wrote a letter to me in which he told this story. The fast-moving, treacherous events had brought a change in his life. Christ had found him and he was a newborn man of faith. He denounced Communism and joined the Christian church. Let me quote for you the last few words of his letter. He said, in closing, "I know now that on that decisive night when I stood with my brother Gabriel in his prison cell it was I who had chosen death — it was Gabriel who had chosen life!"

This is the meaning of this miracle: Our God is an all-loving and all-powerful God. When he is present in the little boat of our life we are never alone, will never be lost and need never fear. For nothing — no force in all the world — is powerful enough to snatch us from his loving and powerful grip.

---

1. William Barclay, *And He Had Compassion* (Valley Forge: Judson Press, 1976), p. 84.

2. Martin Luther, *Sermons on the Gospels*, Vol. II (Rock Island, Illinois: Augustana Book Concern, 1871), p. 262.

3. H. Van der Loos, *The Miracles of Jesus* (London: E. J. Brill, 1968), p. 649.

4. Clovis Chapel, *Sermons From the Miracles* (New York: Abingdon Press), p. 101.

5. Barclay, *op. cit.*, p. 86.

6. Ronald S. Wallace, *The Gospel Miracles* (Grand Rapids, Michigan: William B. Eerdmans Publishing Company, 1960), p. 58.

7. *Ibid.*, p. 59.

8. Martin Luther, *op. cit.*, p. 264.

9. Barclay, *loc. cit.*, p. 86.

Miracle 6

Life Before And After Death

The Raising Of Jairus' Daughter

Matthew 9:18-26; Luke 8:40-56 *(parallel texts)*

This is a story in which devotion and doctrine come together. It is an account of vivid contrasts — human tenderness and profound theology.

It begins with a father's devoted concern for his little daughter and ends with our Lord's tender-hearted sensitivity to a restored child's need for food. Yet, at the same time, in contrast to this touching scene of human emotions, the miracle stands as a sign pointing to the most profound teaching of our faith — the Resurrection, life's victory over death, and the promise of everlasting life.

Compassion is so often mushy, and theology is so often stuffy; but here in a single story the two extremes are woven together harmoniously into an unforgettable story. The human and the divine are combined, and though there are extreme differences involved, there is no resounding clash. For Christ is present and stands in the center of the story. He is the Word become flesh. He is the eternal Holy Word of God revealed in the warm-blooded flesh of the human.

Here in this miracle we are privileged to see "The Gentle Jesus" and "The Cosmic Christ"; our story proclaims that they are one.

The Setting
Jesus is now coming to the close of his Galilean ministry. He has healed the sick, given sight to the blind, healing to the deaf,

hope to the poor and despised. He has proclaimed the Kingdom of God with a courageous conviction that has pleased many, but antagonized some.

He has reached great heights of popularity and at the same time threatened the power structure of the religious leaders who rule in high places. He has revised the Law and broken the sacred Sabbath. To say the least, he has become a controversial figure. To some he is a famous prophet, to others he is an infamous blasphemer.

As our story opens, Jesus is leaving the Eastern shores of Decapolis and sailing toward Capernaum. The lake is small, so the people on the other side soon see his boat and rush to the shore to greet him. And among them — in fact out in front of them all — is a frantic father, Jairus by name, who desperately desires Jesus to help his seriously-ill child.

Jairus

Jairus was ruler of the local synagogue; because of this we can safely assume he was rich, respected, and religious. There is disagreement among interpreters, however, about his exact attitude toward Jesus. We know that, at the time of this miracle story, our Lord had incurred the hatred of many religious leaders. Again and again he had ignored and actually defied the Law by healing on the Sabbath. Hostility against him had become so serious that, prior to our story, Mark records (Mark 3:1-6) that when Jesus had healed the man with a crippled hand in the synagogue on the Sabbath, the Pharisees were furious. Mark ends the account, "So the Pharisees left the synagogue and met at once with some members of Herod's party, and made plans against Jesus to kill him."

Walter Lowrie believes, "Jairus belonged to a class of dignitaries which were generally hostile to Jesus. Jairus, if he was not himself a scribe, must have been in sympathy with the pharisaical party."[1]

Because of this, William Barclay describes Jairus as a man "who was prepared to swallow his pride. He was prepared to ask help from the man he had despised."[2]

Other interpreters like Hendriksen, Nineham, and Ronald Wallace recognize that not all the religious leaders shared the attitude of the Pharisees toward Jesus. Some listened to him and responded positively. As Nineham puts it, "There were those who, when trouble forced them to face realities, could not help admitting power and even begging for its exercise, with a public display of humility which showed that they really recognized its character and source."[3]

Ronald Wallace goes so far as to say, "It was faith that had brought Jairus to Jesus. He believed that this Teacher and Healer could do something for him in his need and despair."[4]

Even though his exact attitude toward Jesus is debated by interpreters, we do know from the plot of the story that Jairus was a devoted father and dearly loved his daughter. Therefore, he was deeply distressed because of her serious illness; so much so that he did an unusual thing for a man in his position. Mark says that when he saw Jesus he threw himself down at his feet and begged him as hard as he could to come and heal his daughter.

It was surprising to behold a man who was looked up to by everyone in the community assuming such an undignified and demeaning position before a young prophet who was in serious trouble with the Pharisees. No wonder Mark, Matthew, and Luke all stress the size of the crowd that thronged about Jesus that day. This was not something seen every day. This drama of Jairus kneeling before Jesus was an event that would make headlines in the daily papers in any age and draw a crowd in any community.

Remembering that Jairus was a rich man, who undoubtedly had utilized all the medical services and resources money could buy, explains to some extent the extraordinary lengths to which Jairus was willing to go. He realized all his prayers in the synagogue and all his influence and wealth accomplished nothing. Jesus was his last and only hope.

Sometimes when we think that money and power and influence can do everything, we need to remember Jairus. He was a man of privilege, but he knew the poverty of privilege when facing life's most perplexing problems. We might drown our sorrows in champagne and stuff ourselves with epicurean delights but still thirst and starve to death, if what we really need is "the water that ends thirst," and "the bread that gives life."

Jesus Makes A House Call

Some of us remember when the family doctor hitched up his horse to a buggy and traveled through the worst kinds of weather to make a house call on one of his sick patients. Today, however, with specialization and the ever-increasing public demand for medical services, this is a drama lost from the American scene.

In this miracle story, our Lord makes a house call. This was not his usual practice. In most cases, patients were carried to him, as today we go to our doctor's office. In some cases Jesus healed from a distance people who were ill at home, without himself going to them. In this situation Jairus begs him to go to his home where his little girl is seriously ill. Mark records that Jesus went with him.

For many interpreters of our miracle this little fact has "deep and significant meaning." Most of us are aware that Christ is present in the church when the worshipers gather each Sunday morning to praise and thank God. We may go to the empty church in time of stress to pray privately because somehow we sense the divine presence within the hallowed walls of "God's House."

Wallace points out, "There is something else that we have yet to discover. He comes here (the church) not only to be able to meet us for a 'brief hour,' but also in order to be able to go with us. He is here so that we can ask him to accompany us on our way home, and on our way into the midst of our trials and anxieties and temptations as he accompanied Jairus."[5]

This is a word of real comfort for us all and gives the human dimension of the Incarnation a home-like setting in our daily lives. God became flesh not simply to die for us, but in order that he might live with us, enter into the most ordinary events of our daily lives. He goes with us into the factory and mill, the office and the supermarket, the school and the shop. He is where we are; and he is there when we need him most.

The major events of our Lord's life centered about ordinary things: a trough, a tree, a trumpet. A feed trough in a cattle barn was his cradle. A tree in the shape of a cross where he suffered stood on a hill beside a garbage dump. The trumpets of Easter with their marvelous message sounded forth from a tomb in a cemetery.

These great events of revelation happened not in the holy sanctuary of a church but in the most ordinary and mundane locations of common life — a barn, a garbage dump, a cemetery.

When Jairus begged our Lord to go home with him, there was no hesitation. Jesus laid down no conditions. Our Lord knew only there was a need, so Jesus went home with Jairus.

Tormenting Delay

No sooner had Jesus started off with Jairus than a woman in the crowd touched Jesus to steal a miracle from him. Our Lord stopped. Some tense moments followed. Jesus spent precious time finding the one who had touched him. Once identified, the woman confessed all and received the full blessing of a complete healing. All this took time — valuable, critical moments that might mean the difference between life and death for Jairus' daughter.

It is not difficult to imagine what must have gone through Jairus' mind. He was fearfully anxious for his daughter's life and now this tormenting delay. Even now it might be too late.

Jairus was beside himself with nervous tension and frustration. But he waited. What else could he do? Viewing this story as a whole, we know that the delay was not decisive. Jesus had the situation well in hand, as he always does.

How many times do we, like Jairus, find ourselves in such a situation? We have a serious problem or a tormenting trouble facing us. We knock and the door does not open. We seek and do not find. We ask and are not given. We plead to our Lord and our prayers are not immediately answered.

At such times we need to remind ourselves of the lesson Jairus learned that day, namely, trust in the Lord, don't rush or push him. He will in his own time accomplish what we need and fulfill our proper desires.

Once there was a king whose only son was seriously ill. The court physicians told the king there was a master of medicine in the East who had the only remedy known to cure the boy's rare disease. The king immediately sent word and implored the medical man to come and cure his son. He agreed.

Anxiously each day the king waited, stood on the castle wall gazing out to sea in hope of sighting the ship from the East. Finally it was sighted and in his excited desperation, the king sent out his navy to urge the approaching ship to greater speed. But frightened by the sight of an armed fleet, and thinking the king's son had died and the ruler was seeking revenge, the approaching ship turned and sailed away.

A few days later, realizing they were not pursued by the king's navy, the ship again returned to the harbor. Once more the impatient king blundered. Completely ignorant of navigation, he gave the wrong signals and the incoming ship was caught in an adverse current and swept back out to sea.

Finally his advisers convinced the king to let the ship arrive in its own way. The king followed their advice, was patient, and no longer interfered. The ship reached the harbor. The remedy was administered to the ailing prince and he was at once cured.

This story is an illustration of the fact that the less we interfere with God's actions the better. He will in his own time, and in his own way, meet our needs, and fulfill our proper desires. Trust God, and all will be well.

So it was Jairus. The tormenting delay did not affect the positive outcome of our miracle story. In the end the little girl was given back to her father as strong and as healthy as ever before.

A Dilemma

The front line in the fight of faith is in many cases not a border between doubt and belief, but it is on a fence located between two possible solutions and is called a "dilemma."

A dilemma is defined as "a choice between alternatives." It is like literally being on a fence trying to decide which way to jump.

One evening a middle-aged man came across a young man climbing up on the railing of a bridge, preparing to jump into the river. The man caught hold of the boy and asked him why he wanted to kill himself. The young man answered, "Life isn't worth living." Then followed a lengthy conversation with both talking at the same time and neither listening to the other. Finally the man said, "Tell you what, give me five minutes to tell you why life is

106

worth living. Then I'll give you give minutes to tell me why life isn't worth living. If at the end of ten minutes, you still want to end your life, I won't stop you."

The young man agreed. Each spoke his allotted time, and at the end of ten minutes, both men climbed up onto the railing and jumped into the river.

Life is somehow like this; given equal time, pessimism seems always to win out over optimism. People tend to believe the worst.

The question of our miracle story is: Would this prove true in the case of Jairus? He was soon to find himself squarely on the fence of a decisive dilemma and the final outcome of the story depends on which way he decides to jump.

When Jesus had cured the woman with the issue of blood and had given her the blessing, "Go in peace," he turned back to Jairus ready to continue their journey. At that very moment some people arrived from Jairus' house with the sad message, "Your daughter has died." Then they add the pessimistic note, "Bother the teacher no longer."

Jairus was shocked, he felt faint, his single thread of hope had suddenly snapped. Jesus, however, ignored the messengers. As Hendricksen so aptly puts it, "With majestic calmness he refused completely to lend an ear to the heralds of doom, the messengers of despair."[6]

Our Lord looked Jairus straight in the eye and said, "Don't be afraid, only believe." It is the typical message of our Lord flowing from the divine optimism of God.

Jairus was understandably confused. His original request to Jesus had been based on the belief that this young man of God had the power to heal his daughter. Now he was being asked to trust in Jesus' power to raise the dead.

What should he do? Whom should he listen to? On the one hand was the plain, practical, but pessimistic message of his friends, "It's all over; your daughter is dead!" On the other hand was the hopeful and optimistic word from Jesus, "Fear not. Only believe!"

On either side of his dilemma-fence were those who wanted to help. His friends were natural-born pessimists, but they were also practical men of common sense. They were decent men and had no desire to intentionally hurt Jairus. They took no joy in being the bearers of bad news.

These men wanted Jairus, according to Wallace, to "face up to life with all its stark realities, and with all the possibilities it holds of failure and death. Face it bravely and squarely. If you have had it, you have had it, and you must take it like a man."[7]

Sherman Johnson sees here a "touch of dramatic irony; they do not realize the depths of Jesus' compassion which is that of God, or his power to act even when everything seems lost."[8]

On the other hand stood Christ. He had heard the same message Jairus had heard, that the girl was dead; yet he still persisted in continuing the journey of healing. It could mean only one thing; this Jesus of Nazareth was making the claim that his help did not cease at the point of death. This was a fantastic assumption. No man could raise the dead.

If Jairus listened to Jesus and followed him home, would he be opening himself up to ridicule by his friends and public accusations that he was a stupid fool — a religious radical who in his moment of grief had gone mad? Jairus had to decide whether to follow the pessimistic but practical, common-sense way of the world that says "death" is the final word, or to follow after Jesus and the optimistic and fantastic claim that "death" is not the last word.

Is this not where we find ourselves? There is the practical common-sense point of view that death is the end. We have our day and then cease to be. As in a ball game, the whistle blows and it is all over. There is no chance to change the score or capture the trophy. This is the view of secular science that exercises such control over our thoughts and life. Existence is a natural biological process and death is the only and absolute end. It all sounds so much in agreement with our experiences of life and death.

Over against all the evidence that the pessimists are right, one optimistic promise is heard: "I am the resurrection and the life. Whoever believes in me will live, even though he dies; and whoever lives and believes in me will not die" (John 11:25, 26).

Our problem is not so much a matter of dispelling doubt as deciding whom to believe, whom to listen to. Our dilemma is increased because neither side can offer absolute proof — evidence perhaps, but not proof. It finally comes down to taking that jump from the "dilemma-fence," leaping either in the direction of the world of common sense or in the direction of the Word of Christ our Savior.

The answer our miracle story gives is found in the action of Jairus. He decides to follow Jesus. His reaction is an interesting one. According to the record, he doesn't say anything. He doesn't argue with his friends. He doesn't make any great claim of faith or confession of belief to Jesus. Jairus simply jumps down from the fence of his dilemma and follows after Jesus.

Thereon hangs the thread of our story. In his hour of crisis, Jairus remains in the presence of Jesus. He may not fully believe that this strange young man can raise his daughter from the dead. He has made no commitment to faith in Christ's power to do the impossible. But he remains in the presence of Christ — he follows after Jesus, and as we shall see later, this is decisive in understanding the meaning and message of the miracle story.

The Chosen Three

The first thing that Jesus does is to dismiss the crowd. Mark writes, "Then he did not let anyone go on with him except Peter, James, and his brother John." These were the same three Christ chose to experience the Transfiguration and to go with him to the Garden where he struggled in prayer with the reality of his coming crucifixion and death.

One explanation for this action of selecting just three of his disciples is that, in Jewish thought, based on the law, two or three witnesses were required to validate an event (Deuteronomy 19:15). The miracle event which was about to happen would thereby be validated, at least in the Jewish minds, by the presence of the three witnesses.

Lowrie sees this requirement for three witnesses reflected in the statement made in Matthew, "Where two or three come together in my name, I am there with them" (Matthew 18:20). This presents the viewpoint of most interpreters who see the presence of the chosen three as not only a validating of the miracle event, but Mark's way of assuring his readers that Christ was truly present when the daughter of Jairus was raised from the dead.

Here again we have a detail suggesting that the *presence of Jesus* is important to discovering the message and meaning of this miracle.

Another Crowd Dismissed

Jesus had just dismissed one crowd, then he arrived at the home of Jairus and encountered yet another. This was a crowd of professional mourners, minstrels, and concerned neighbors.

The *Talmud* and custom demanded that at the time of death the poorest Israelite should have at least two flute-players and at least one female mourner who would chant a lamentation for the dead. Alois Stoger tells us that "this was sung in the form of a responsory, to the accompaniment of hand clapping, the beat of tambourines and wooden clappers."[9]

W. M. Thomson remarks about these professional women mourners, "They know the domestic history of every person and immediately strike up an impromtu lamentation, in which they introduce the names of their relatives who have recently died, touching some tender chord in every heart."[10]

The flute-players, or as Matthew refers to them, "the minstrels," were an integral part of mourning in every country in ancient times. The number of howling women mourners, flute-players, tambourines, and clappers increased in proportion to the wealth and social standing of the grieving family. Since Jairus was a rich and influential leader in the community, what greeted Jesus as he approached the house must have been sheer pandemonium. As one of my students described it, "It sounded much like a gathering of hard-rock groups at a festival in Woodstock."

How Jesus ever brought all this confusion, loud crying, and wailing to a halt would seem like a minor miracle in itself. But he did. And he sent them all away.

Some have interpreted Jesus' sending the mourners away as an attack on the extremes of contemporary funeral arrangements and practices, where the realities of death are not honestly faced but expensively avoided. They point out that undertakers are trained to hide and disguise the reality of death. Artificiality is the mark of their professional skill to make the dead look alive. We respond to their successful efforts with the approving comment, "They look so natural."

Cemeteries become parks of green lawns, or slumber rooms where soft music creates an atmosphere of tranquility and eternal bliss. No judgment here; only a comment that someone cares. Perpetual care comes to mean not a continuing concern but an embalmed moment, frozen in time, so that the state of one's existence is suspended in a non-real void somewhere between time and eternity — a perpetual purgatory of preservation.

A case can be made that Jesus, in this action of driving the mourners from the house of Jairus, is attacking the artificial paraphernalia of mourning commonly used in his day. Obviously this is not a scene of honest grief but a spectacle — a theatrical performance. Jesus deplores such, wherever and under whatever circumstances he uncovered "dead bones in white boxes."

Supporting this assumption that Jesus is making a social statement by his treatment of the mourners is the reaction of the mourners to his statement, "The child is not dead — she is only sleeping." Matthew, Mark, and Luke all point out that immediately the mourners, "made fun of him." They ridiculed and laughed in his face.

Lane finds this significant. "The fact that wailing and tears could be exchanged so quickly for laughter indicates how conventional and artificial the mourning customs had become."[11]

Other interpreters have seen in Christ's driving the mourners from the scene the disapproval of our Lord for all forms of grief at the time of death. Barclay, for example, believes that one of the two "eternal truths" of this story is that there is no cause for mourning at the time of death. He says, "When someone dies it is natural and inevitable to be sad, but our sorrow is for ourselves and not for those who have died. If we believe that death is only a sleep from which we wake to be in heaven, we cannot be sorry for those who have died. So far from being sorry, we ought to be glad that they have entered into a far greater life."[12]

Today outward expressions of emotion are considered to be an important part of the grief process. They are the means by which we are enabled to accept the fact of death and adjust ourselves to the resulting loss of a loved one. It appears inconsistent with the total biblical witness that Jesus is here discouraging all human expressions of grief, for the shortest verse in the Bible tells us that at the death of his friend Lazarus "Jesus wept" (John 11:35).

When all the evidence is in, Schnackenburg would seem to present the most reasonable and acceptable interpretation of Jesus' reaction to the mourners. He does not see Jesus making any moral or ethical judgments on the grief process, nor presenting any "eternal truths" concerning a Christian reaction or attitude toward the experience of the death situation. Schnackenburg simply sees Jesus removing the wailing women and flute-players "for the purpose of performing the miracle in quietness and secret."[13]

Jesus had no intention of performing a miracle in front of a raucous crowd of unbelievers who ridiculed him and laughed in his face then, and he has no intention of doing so now. Miracles have meaning and a message only for those who, in faith, believe in him.

Little Girl! Get Up!

When the crowd left and only the chosen three disciples and Jairus remained, Jesus walked over to the bed where the child lay and said, "Talitha koum." Mark adds, "which means, 'Little girl! Get up, I tell you!' "

Scholars disagree about how this added translation of the Aramaic term is to be interpreted. Most of them believe Mark gives a Greek translation for the sake of his Roman readers who would not have understood the Aramaic. Others see the added translation as evidence that Jesus is using an incantation which was typical of the miracle workers of his day.

Origen, speaking to the question of why Mark adds the translation, points out that it is well known that spells and incantations lose their power when translated into another language. Mark is therefore prohibiting future faith healers from using this incantation for their own. Rawlinson agrees, "It is to guard against such an idea that the Evangelist deliberately translates them."[14]

Lane speaks against an "incantation-theory." He states, "There is no evidence that 'Talitha cumi' or 'Ephphatha' were ever used by Christian healers as a magical spell."[15] In the light of Origen's comment, this is precisely the point. The words were never used by Christian healers as an incantation because the translation of these words by the Gospel writers made the words ineffective as incantations.

Hendriksen gives the most plausible interpretation to the use of the words "Talitha koum" by stating that our Lord was addressing the little girl in her own native tongue, "using the very words by means of which her mother had probably often awakened her in the morning, namely, 'Talitha koum.' "[16]

This interpretation agrees with and fits into the tender, home-like atmosphere which pervades the concluding aspects of the miracle story.

Not Dead — Only Sleeping

The cause of all the laughter and ridicule by the professional mourners is that Jesus said, "The child is not dead — she is only sleeping."

This word "sleep" has caused not laughter but serious concern for interpreters. Van der Loos says that, "The word used here occurs in the New Testament in three different meanings: it means sleep in the literal sense, sleep in the figurative sense, and sleep in the sense of being dead."[17]

The question is: What understanding of the word "sleep" did Jesus have in mind when he spoke this word, and what was Mark's understanding of the word when he recorded it? For many scholars this question is crucial because the issue of whether or not the child was actually dead when Christ entered the home depends upon the interpretation given to Jesus' and Mark's use of the word "sleep."

We could at this point in our discussion engage in a lengthy review of the many arguments put forth by scholars on both sides of the issue. But since even today with our mechanical "life support systems" and discussions of "clinical death" and "legal death," we cannot agree as to an exact definition of death, little would be gained by traveling through the critical discussions presented by the various interpreters.

There is little doubt Mark presents here a miracle of the raising of the dead. The issue of whether the child was actually dead or in a coma is beside the point for our purpose. Our concern is: what message and meaning does Jesus' raising of Jairus' daughter have for us today?

Presuppositions

Before considering the message of the miracle, two presuppositions should be established.

Triple Tradition

First, there are only three raisings of the dead in the four Gospels: the raising of Lazarus, the widow's son at Nain, and Jairus' daughter.

Laidlaw is convinced the miracle of Jairus' daughter "should take precedence in this group"[18] because it alone belongs to the "Triple Tradition," meaning that Matthew, Mark, and Luke all have an account of the same miracle. Matthew's account is brief. Luke's record is somewhat longer. Mark presents the most detailed account. At the essential points of the story all three are in agreement as to what happened. All three present this as a miracle of raising a child from the state of death.

Resuscitation

The second presupposition is: The miracle of raising Jairus' daughter was not a resurrection from the dead, but a resuscitation back to life. The young girl is brought back to life as it was before she dies.

Edward Schweizer writes, "The resuscitation of a corpse and the person's return to what for all practical purposes is the same kind of an earthly life ... is the exact opposite of what the Bible calls resurrection — re-creation by God to an existence which is entirely new."[19]

Resurrection as understood by the New Testament writers involves a radical change. As a caterpillar is changed into a butterfly, so we are changed. Our old body returns to the earth from which it came and we are given a new and glorified body. At the same time we are given a new life. God does not restore us to what we were; he makes of us a new creation.

Jesus, in speaking of his own death says, "The hour has now come for the Son of Man to be given great glory. I tell you the truth: a grain of wheat is no more than a single grain unless it is dropped into the ground and dies. If it does die then it produces many grains" (John 12:24). The picture of a seed buried in the ground and then emerging in the new shape and form of a tender plant is what is understood within the New Testament as the experience of dying and being given new life. As a seed differs from a flower, so our present bodies will differ from the glorified body we are to receive.

This was not true in the case of Jairus' daughter. Her experience was not that of sprouting forth in a new form to live a new life. When raised from the dead by Jesus, Jairus' daughter resumed her previous life with all its limitations, including the necessity of eventually facing death and dying again.

What we have therefore in this miracle is an example of life restored and not an *experience* of the resurrection. At best, the event is, in the words of Schnackenburg, a "symbolic imitation"[20] of the coming resurrection event, but not an experience of it.

The miracle of Christ's raising the daughter of Jairus is a sign that Christ has *power* over death, but it is not a revelation that Christ has *overcome* death. The defeat of death is alone accomplished by the cross-event and the resurrection-experience of Easter morn.

We have the promise of eternal life not because Christ has power over death, as exhibitied in the miracle of Jairus' daughter; rather we are given new life by the cross and Resurrection where Christ overcomes death itself. It is at the cross on a hill and from an empty tomb in a garden that our promise of resurrection and new life are given to us.

In this miracle story, Jairus' daughter is resuscitated and thus must die again. In the miracle of the cross and resurrection, we are resurrected and shall never die, but have life eternally with God. This is a decisive difference.

The Presence

Then what does this miracle story say to us? In general, it points to the vital importance of the presence of Christ if we are to experience and possess life. Christ says, "I am the life"; and because he is life, we can have life.

The miracle story shows that Christ takes death seriously. He understands Jairus' concern for his daughter. Our Lord responds to this father's plea for help and goes with him all the way. When the negative message comes that the girl is dead and the friends of Jairus attempt to persuade him that the death is final, Jesus stands with Jairus and comforts and encourages him with a word of hope, "Don't be afraid, only believe."

Jesus does not stop with a word of promise. He acts. He accompanies Jairus to his home, right into the midst of all the stark realities, the clamor and confusion of the death situation. Our Lord sends the wailing mourners away with the word that she is not dead — only asleep. Our Lord remains with Jairus, enters with him into the room where death has driven its deadly blow. Jesus takes the girl by the hand and speaks, "Little girl. Get up, I tell you." The girl gets up and walks around.

Then Mark says, "They were completely amazed." Even in the midst of this amazement, Jesus still remains with the family and gives the practical advice to feed the child.

The one consistent and continuing thread that runs through this miracle story is that Jesus is present with Jairus during the entire ordeal — the serious illness with its threat of death, the experience of death, and then of life restored.

Life Before And After Death

The meaning received from this miracle is a twofold message. It speaks of the effect the presence of Christ has on our life before as well as after death.

116

Life After Death

First the miracle is a sign indicating that as we know Jesus as our Lord and Savior we shall one day know him as the Cosmic Christ. When we face death and are placed in the grave, we will be raised up at the Day of Resurrection and recognize that our Lord has overcome the last and greatest enemy of God, death. And by this victory we are not only given a new and resurrected life, but the whole world has become a new creation.

This is as yet but a promise, a certain hope, an assurance that for us, who are in Christ Jesus, there is a glorified life after death, and we shall live it in a newly-created world.

As important as this promise of a new life and a new creation is, in the miracle of the raising of Jairus' daughter, it is the secondary meaning. The primary message is: there is life *before* death. For those who are in Christ, there is life not only after death but before death.

Life Before Death

The fact has been stressed that the raising of Jairus' daughter was an event of resuscitation, not an event of resurrection. As the meaning of this miracle possesses a twofold message, so we face a twofold problem. There is the problem of what happens to us after we die, but also the problem of what happens to us *before* we die.

We may experience a twofold death. There is the final, physical death of the body that we must all face. But there is also the possibility of being dead before we die. It is the experience of only existing but not really living. Existence is meaningless without purpose. It is lonely and desperate without hope. We walk through life as if we were already dead, for we are not living, only existing.

Alexander King has written a book titled *Is There Life After Birth?* This has been the perplexing question of the existentialists, who for the most part have concluded the existential answer is "No!" Life has no inherent value. Life is meaningless, leading nowhere. We begin dying the moment we are born and all life is death.

One of my students tells about his little boy who got the words of his bedtime prayer mixed up. One night he said, "If I should wake before I die." For many people this is the prayer that plagues their daily life of desperation and drudgery. They ask, "When shall I awake from this nightmare of trouble and suffering? Will I ever get a chance to really live before I die?"

A new lady in the community visited a local church. The topic of the pastor's sermon was "Will we know each other in heaven?" After the service nobody spoke to the visitor, acknowledged her, or even noticed that she was there. When she got home, she wrote a short note to the minister of the church:

> *Last Sunday I attended your church and listened attentively to your sermon. I heard all that you said, but after what I experienced, being a stranger in your congregation, I suggest that next Sunday you preach on the topic "Will we know each other here on earth?"*

Loneliness can be a kind of living death, as can heartache, meaninglessness, depression, disappointment, and suffering. The feeling of being useless, unwanted, and unloved can often be worse than actual death. Our miracle story speaks to this kind of death. It says the presence of Christ promises us not only a resurrection from the grave of final death, but also a resuscitation from a lifeless existence before death. It is a promise that there is life both *before* and *after* death.

This is a great comfort to all of us who are searching to find life before we die. At the same time, it is a challenge to us as church congregations to create an atmosphere in which people might come and experience the presence of a Lord who loves the lonely, the unloved, the troubled. We create such an atmosphere when we extend the hand of friendship and concern to every stranger who comes among us.

This does not mean that sometimes contrived bit of action of turning around and shaking-hands-with-your-neighbor, sometimes called "the Peace." There is nothing wrong with this, except when it becomes a substitute, as it often does, for a sincere openness on the part of the congregation to warmly greet and welcome strangers within its midst.

As we have stressed above, the presence of Christ with Jairus all through his troubles is the vital thread which holds the miracle story together. This presence of Christ today is communicated to those outside of Christ by those who are within Christ. The church is today the Body of Christ. We need to make our Lord's presence known in the lives of others by our sincere concern and care for them, particularly when they, like Jairus, are faced with humbling circumstances — loneliness, depression, disappointment, suffering, and the frightening fear of death.

In a small mid-western town, a man was found dead in a deserted alley. The police quickly apprehended a man running away from the scene of the crime and he was brought to trial. The defense attorney took a most unusual approach. He challenged the State to prove that a person had actually been murdered by producing the identity of the murdered victim.

The State responded immediately, attempting to identify the victim. After months of delays and postponements, the State finally admitted to the court they could not identify the murdered man, or prove by any witnesses that the man had ever been alive. The judge dismissed the case until such time as the victim could be identified.

During the lengthy and unusual trial, the newspapers referred to it as "The Case of the Dead Man Who Never Lived."

Is this not the sad and tragic epitaph of so many people — people we pass by every day on the streets, and in our offices, and in the stores where we shop, and perhaps even in the places where we worship? They will die without ever having lived. Why? Because we failed to share with them the presence of the living Lord.

Paul writes, "For me to live is Christ." That is the primary message of our miracle story: the presence of Christ and his promise that there is life *before* as well as *after* death. For all who surrender and trust in the Lord, to them is given life, an abundant, full, meaningful life, both now before death and later after death.

But for the Jairuses and little girls ill at home today, how shall they come to know the presence of Christ if we are silent and fail to share with them that presence of the living Lord so freely given to us? Pray God that somehow through us a few more might come to know Christ and experience life *before* as well as *after* death.

119

1. Walter Lowrie, *Jesus According to St. Mark* (London: Longmans, Green and Company, 1929), p. 219.

2. William Barclay, *And He Had Compassion* (Valley Forge: Judson Press, 1975), p. 105.

3. D. E. Nineham, *The Gospel of St. Mark, The Pelican Commentaries* (New York: The Seabury Press, 1963), p. 157.

4. Ronald S. Wallace, *The Gospel Miracles* (Grand Rapids, Michigan: William B. Eerdmans Publishing Comany, 1960), p. 75.

5. *Ibid.*, p. 74.

6. William Hendriksen, *Exposition of the Gospel According to Mark,* New Testament Commentary (Grand Rapids, Michigan: Baker Book House, 1975), p. 211.

7. Wallace, *op. cit.*, p. 224.

8. Sherman Johnson, *A Commentary on the Gospel According to St. Mark* (New York: Harper and Brothers Publishers, 1960), p. 108.

9. Lowrie, *op. cit.*, p. 224.

10. Alois Stoger, *The Gospel According to St. Luke* (New York: Herder and Herder, 1969), p. 165.

11. W. M. Thompson, *The Land and the Book*, quoted in Barclay, *op. cit.*, p. 103.

12. William L. Lane, *The Gospel According to Mark* (Grand Rapids, Michigan: William B. Eerdmans Publishing Company, 1974), p. 197.

13. Barclay, *op. cit.*, p. 113.

14. Rudolf Schnackenburg, *The Gospel According to St. Mark* (New York: Herder and Herder, 1971), p. 93.

15. A. E. J. Rawlinson, *St. Mark* (London: Methuen and Company, Ltd., 1942), p. 72.

16. Lane, *op. cit.*, p. 198.

17. Hendriksen, *op. cit.*, p. 214.

18. H. Van der Loos, *The Miracles of Jesus* (Leiden: E. J. Brill, 1968), p. 568.

19. John Laidlaw, *The Miracles of Our Lord* (Grand Rapids, Michigan: Baker Book House, 1956), p. 338.

20. Edward Schweizer, *The Good News According to Mark* (Atlanta, Georgia: John Knox Press, 1976), p. 121.

Miracle 6 – Alternate

The Woman Who Attempted To Steal A Miracle

The Woman With An Issue Of Blood

Matthew 9:18-26; Luke 8:40-56 *(parallel texts)*

Pick up the morning newspaper and you are certain to be confronted by another crime committed. And it seems that one crime is more bizarre than the other. The miracle we now consider is an account of a strange and unusual crime. It is the story of a woman who attempted to steal a miracle.

In many ways, this woman was like the leper who was cured and sent to the priest. Both were untouchables and lived lonely, desperate lives. Just as today our lives are controlled by computers and their printouts, so in the days of our Lord people's lives were controlled by the holy Law. And under this law the woman with an issue of blood, as well as the leper, was forbidden to mingle with people in public places. So they both broke the law by entering into the gathering that surrounded Jesus.

However, they solved their problems in vastly different ways. The leper stormed the kingdom with violence. This woman eased her way into the kingdom unnoticed. She was quiet and secretive. But then she could be, for her disease, unlike leprosy, was not outwardly apparent. If the people had known about her affliction, they would have avoided her as they did the leper.

Her plan was simple. She would hide herself in the crowd, and when no one was looking, she would touch just the fringe of his garment, steal a little bit of his power, just enough to be healed,

123

and then withdraw from the crowd as she had entered it, quietly and secretively. Part of her plan worked. But she was caught and exposed. To her surprise, and to ours, she was not punished for her assault on the personhood of Jesus, but she was declared to be a woman of faith. And therein we find the plot of our story and the message it proclaims.

Religious Attitude Or Faith

Before we consider the details of this miracle, we need to come to terms with the meaning and use of the word "faith." Commentators and interpreters, all through their discussions of this miracle, refer to the "faith" of this woman. They point out that it is an immature faith, a faith based on superstition and belief in magical powers. Their use of the term "faith" can be misleading. The mindset of this woman at the beginning of the story is far from what the New Testament means when it talks about faith. It will be much more helpful for our discussion of this miracle to refer to the *religious attitude* of this woman when she came to Jesus rather than her *faith*.

Wallace, in describing the scene that day when the miracle happened, pictures thronging crowds that crushed in upon Jesus. Many who pushed in on him had troubles and problems almost as serious as the woman's, but as Wallace observes, "This woman alone had the attitude toward Jesus which enabled him to meet her personal need."[1] She of all the people in the crowd "touched" Jesus. Not just physically, but in a far more profound sense. As Saint Augustine puts it, "Many thronged him, one touched him."

What was this religious attitude she exhibited toward Jesus? First, it was an attitude of fear. And much of what we call religion begins with fear. The lightning strikes, and the thunder rumbles through the sky, and primitive man searches out a god to protect him. His crops fail, or his herds become diseased and die, or hunting becomes difficult, and he searches for a god to help him. He looks for a god of good power to protect and help him from the evil forces of bad power. Such was the attitude of this woman. She was driven by fear and desperation to the point of despair. She needed to find some power greater than the evil powers that had invaded and possessed her body.

Second, she heard about Jesus as a man possessing unusual power. Perhaps she had even seen him cure others. As she watched him reach forth his hand and touch the afflicted and saw that they were instantly healed, she became convinced that she must somehow plug in on this power.

Third, and perhaps the most revealing of all, her attitude says that somehow he had that power within himself. He was not calling on some god to bless the patient; he was himself the source of the power that healed.

Most of those who gathered about Jesus viewed him as a special prophet in touch with the God their people had so long worshiped — the God of Abraham, Isaac, and Jacob. When he spoke in the synagogue, they were impressed that he spoke as one with authority. Some even thought he was the Messiah sent from God to be their great deliverer, but they never thought of him as a god.

The woman with the issue of blood, on the other hand, saw Jesus not just as a man of authority but of divine power. She certainly did not understand the complex concept of the Incarnation; yet the details given in the account do suggest that in a primitive sense, her approach toward Jesus was as if he were god-like. Her belief in the power of Jesus was at the level of magic and superstition. Nonetheless, she possessed a religious attitude that this man was more than just a man; he was a holy man of power. That is why she reasoned, if only she could get near enough to touch him, to make contact with the magical god-like power he possessed, she could be healed.

Of course this attitude is far from what the New Testament understands as *faith* — even imperfect faith. Faith, in the Bible, has to do with a personal relationship between God and his people. In the Old Testament it was spoken of in terms of covenant, an agreement between God and his chosen people. This woman's attitude toward Jesus was completely and exclusively in the realm of *power*. There was nothing *personal* in her attitude toward Jesus. She did not want to know him, or follow him, or have fellowship with him. She didn't even want to be noticed by him. All she wanted was to get in close to him, get a cure, and get out as quickly as possible.

As Wallace observes, "This woman made a very serious error in her attitude to Jesus as she came up to him in the crowd. She wanted only healing and strength from him but not personal love."[2]

Therefore, it is necessary in the understanding of this miracle to see this woman's actions as the result not of faith, even imperfect faith, but the result of a religious attitude marked by superstition and belief in magical power.

This realization could be important for us as well, because we might come to recognize that much we identify as faith within ourselves is not faith at all but simply the same religious attitude this woman possessed concerning *power*. Do we want just the power of God without commitment, surrender, and involvement with Christ personally? Do we view worship and prayer as means of plugging into the source of divine power rather than personal communion with our living Lord?

If we do hold such an attitude sometimes, this miracle offers us a word of hope. For it is the story of a woman who starts out with a religious attitude of superstition but is changed by her experience with Jesus to become a woman of faith.

Her Problem

Mark begins the story with the words, "There was a woman." We could stop here and say that this woman had a problem. In the male-dominated world in which she lived, being a woman made her, at the very best, a second-class citizen. It was a culture in which every night each little Jewish lad thanked God in his prayers that he was not a girl! As Hendriksen points out, "At that time, and in that country, for a woman to speak in public was generally considered most improper."[3]

She was not only a woman, but she was a woman suffering from a severe bleeding for twelve long years. Scholars attempt to identify this malady as everything from a bleeding ulcer to cancer of the colon. But as Lenski indicates, "None of the evangelists says enough about her ailment so that we can determine its exact nature."[4]

126

We do know that she had gone to many doctors who had relieved her only of her money. She was not only sick but broke when she came to Jesus. And instead of getting better, each day her condition became worse.

Hendriksen sums it up, "It would seem, however, that the best answer to the question why this woman was not healed is given by the man who himself was a doctor, namely, Luke who plainly states that her illness was humanly speaking, and in the light of the therapeutic of that day, incurable" (Luke 8:43).[5]

On top of all this, she was religiously unclean. Barclay comments, "The real tragedy of an illness like that was that, according to the Jewish law, it made a woman unclean."[6] Leviticus 15:25-27, as all the law does, spells it out very much to the point:

> *Every bed on which she lies, all the days of her discharge, shall be to her as the bed of her impurity; and everything on which she sits shall be unclean, as in the uncleaness of her impurity. And whoever touches these things shall be unclean, and shall wash his clothes and bathe himself in water, and be unclean until the evening.*

She could not attend the synagogue or associate with her friends and relatives. Condemned by ritual law and the priestly cult, she could touch no one and no one could touch her. She was literally cut off from all social and religious life.

In Morris West's novel, *The Shoes of the Fisherman*, there is an incident in which the Pope goes into the poor section of Rome incognito. He is about to enter a house where a man has just died to bring what comfort he can to the family. He is greeted at the door by a young woman who tells him he is really not needed now, for as she says, "They can cope with death. It is only living that defeats them."

This was the condition of the woman in our miracle story. Life was in the process of defeating her. So far as society was concerned, she was like one dead. And there must have been many moments when she felt it would be better if she were dead. But then things changed; she heard about Jesus.

She Heard

Mark continues his story, "She heard about Jesus." It is interesting that in each of the miracle stories, the turning point of the patient's life is the time when someone tells them about Jesus. Suddenly the helpless condition of the person in need is transfused with hope.

Many interpreters point to the determination of this lady, born out of desperation, as the most important factor in bringing her to Jesus. The text, however, supports the fact it was a word — a word spoken to her by unnamed friends. The story that followed would never have happened without that word of witness. The implication of the story is that this woman was at the end of her rope; when she heard about Jesus, she tied a knot in that rope and decided to hold on to the possibility that he might be the answer to all her hopes and prayers.

Pearl Buck tells of a custom in China of giving to one's friends a beautifully decorated porcelain dish with a gracefully designed lid. It is filled with candy which is eaten by the receiver. But then custom demands that the dish be refilled with sweets and given as a gift to someone else. Thus the receiving of a gift makes of each friend a potential giver.

So it is with the Word. Having heard, we are made potential tellers of the Word. Thus an unending chain is formed which reaches out to touch another and another until all have heard and that chain encircles the whole earth with the glorious good news of God's grace.

How many miracles of faith never happen because we are silent and break the chain! Because we fail to share our faith, many people are condemned to live empty, desperate, and hopeless lives.

She Talked To Herself

The text states that, before the woman came to Jesus, she talked to herself. Clovis Chappell is impressed with this detail. He points out that "what we say to each other is sometimes important, but what we say to ourselves is always crucial."[7] Here the woman says to herself, "If I touch just his clothes, I shall get well." To Chappell this statement is crucial, for it shows that the word is working in her life.

"If" is an open attitude that brings hope and leads to faith. By this we know that she did not doubt the word she heard, nor did she ignore it. The word was within her and it had taken root. But the full promise of the word still waited to be fulfilled. Would it grow and blossom into faith? That for Clovis Chappell was the decisive question and issue of the miracle.

However, when we note exactly what it was she said to herself, the future of her becoming a woman of faith seems not very promising. She said, "If I touch *just* his clothes." This indicates that even at this stage, her actions are being motivated by a religious attitude dominated by magic and superstition.

She Touched His Cloak

Embarrassed because of her unclean condition, she did not dare confront our Lord with her need. Her plan was to become lost in the crowd and when the chance presented itself to touch just the edge of his cloak. Matthew and Luke both say, "The edge of his cloak." Sometimes the words "fringe" or "hem" are used to describe this edge. Mark simply says, "His cloak."

Most scholars agree that what is intended here is to indicate she touched the "tassels" [*tsitsith*] which had symbolic significance.

Jesus more than likely wore a *shimla* which was a square cloth used as an outer robe. At each of the four corners of the *shimla* hung a tassel required by the ritualistic law of Deuteronomy 22:12. These tassels had a double purpose; they identified the person as a Jew to strangers and reminded the Jew who wore them of his heritage as a chosen child of God.

Lenski points out that "the Pharisees loved to make these conspicuous in order to display their compliance with the law."[8]

Customarily two corners of the *shimla* were thrown back over the shoulders so that two of the tassels hung down in the back and swung freely as the person walked. So it is easy to imagine how the woman thought she could touch just one of these tassels and make contact with the healing power of Jesus without his noticing it.

Fringe Areas Of Faith

We might pause here to indicate that many homileticians have been attracted to this specific action of the woman in touching just the fringe area of our Lord's garment. They find in this a stimulating symbol of many people today in the church who live at the "fringe areas of faith."

Back in the Middle Ages people would steal holy water from the font and bread from the altar, using these in their rites of black magic and witchcraft because of the "power" they believed these elements possessed. They conceived of this power as neutral, able to be used for good or bad purposes, to curse or to bless.

Today many preachers believe that people often confuse a religious power-attitude with faith. The worshiper thinks a kind of "holy magic" exists within the sacraments of Communion and Baptism. They are the people one theologian has referred to as "sprinkled Christians." They want the church to sprinkle them with *water* when they are born, with *rice* when they are married, and with *dirt* when they die.

By these ritualistic practices, these fringe-followers of Christ feel somehow they are blessed and protected from the evil forces of our world regardless of any personal involvement with the living Lord. When communion is offered, they take it as one would a prescription of medicine. It is a pill possessing the potential power of grace.

Even the Bible as a holy book can become a fetish. Many think that having a Bible in the house, displayed in a prominent place, augments their policy with "All State" and gives them added "hands" of protection.

At a revival service, one man testified that the Bible had actually saved his life. He told that his mother had given him a little copy of the New Testament when he went off to war. He always carried it in his shirt pocket over his heart. One day during battle, a piece of shrapnel hit him directly in the chest and lodged in the copy of the New Testament. He stated, "If it hadn't been for that copy of the New Testament, I would be a dead man today!"

Now that is true, but one is tempted to add that an unabridged copy of *Webster's Dictionary* would have given him even greater protection.

We can smile at such a story, but how many of us, if we are truly honest with ourselves, partake of the sacraments, attend services of worship, and form habits of prayer not motivated by faith as much as by a religious attitude of fear — fear that is more akin to superstition than to faith — fear that if we fail to do certain rituals we open ourselves up to evil forces of fate waiting to attack us.

Superstition Not All Bad

We need to remind ourselves, however, that superstition has often been the seed bed of faith. Most superstitions were born out of the realization that we are not our own masters. The realization that there are forces and powers beyond our control which shape and form our destinies directs us to look outside ourselves for help — and this is good. The destructive counterside of faith is not religious power — attitudes or belief in magic and superstition as much as the prideful belief in ourselves. When we think we need no outside help because we are perfectly capable of dealing with everything that confronts us, then we are in trouble. When we think we need nothing but ourselves, then we are on the road to pure secularism which is the greatest threat to possessing true faith in our contemporary world.

The person who is superstitious at least realizes that he desperately needs help from outside himself. And that can create fertile ground, receptive to the word about power coming to him from beyond himself. Superstition, with its attempt to reach beyond itself and outside itself, is a possible receptive soil for planting the seeds of a true faith in God.

Therefore, it is better to practice the rituals of worship superstitiously rather than not at all. The tragedy is that we stop at this level of belief and fail to permit religious power-attitudes to give way to faith born of a Word from God.

No Hero Of The Faith

It is safe to assume that the woman of our miracle story was no hero of the faith. Actually she was a criminal to the faith. She committed a horrible crime against the innocent bystanders and this man called Jesus.

131

She had pushed her way into the crowd and contaminated each person she touched. She broke serious rules of her society and her Temple. She did not know that Jesus was the Christ, the Savior of her people, but she did know that he was a good man who had helped and healed many people. However, in her selfish desire to acquire a cure for herself, she had dared to touch this holy man.

Her touch contaminated Jesus more than ritualistically. In those days it was believed that the only way a disease could be cured was for its contamination to flow into the person of another. Animals were frequently used for this purpose, as when Jesus drove the evil spirits out of the demoniac and into the swine.

Therefore, she was actually transferring her plague to the personhood of Jesus. Maybe she didn't realize the full implications of her actions; yet what her action meant was, "Better he have the plague than me." True, as many commentators stress, she was a woman of determination, but her determination was selfish and self-centered and certainly not a virtue to be emulated or admired.

Power Gone Out Of Him

The moment Jesus was touched by the woman, Mark states, "At once Jesus felt that power had gone out of him."

This detail of the story has caused great concern for scholars. How is this action to be interpreted and what is the meaning of this word "power"?

It was a popular belief in the time of Jesus that the dignity and power of a person were transferred to what he wore. The woman's desire to touch Jesus' clothing probably reflects this quasi-magical notion. But Mark states that it was Jesus who felt that power had gone out of him. What then did Jesus mean by this?

Lowrie concludes that "the fact that he (Jesus) usually effected his cures by some sort of physical contact suggests that he was conscious of a healing power going out of him."[9] This would mean that every time Jesus cured a person there was this same feeling, but only in this particular case did he mention it because of the unusual nature of the healing.

Such a suggestion really creates more questions than it answers. All we can conclude from the content of the text is that somehow this woman made contact by her touch with the power Jesus possessed.

Lane suggests that Jesus possessed the power of God as the representative of the Father. However, the Father retained control of this power, even though it resided in Jesus and could be used by him in his acts of healing. Lane therefore concludes that "the healing of the woman occurred through God's free and gracious decision to bestow upon her the power which was active in Jesus. By an act of sovereign will God determined to honor the woman's faith in spite of the fact that it was tinged with ideas which bordered on magic."[10]

This explanation is helpful for two reasons. First, it avoids the superstitious idea that there was a nimbus of holy presence that surrounded Jesus and which mechanically and automatically cured any who stepped within its sphere.

Second, it is helpful to understand Christ's statement that it was her faith that made her well. If the faith Christ is referring to is the result of God giving his own power into her life, then we can understand why a woman who lacked any faith of her own and possessed only a religious attitude tinged with magic and superstition when she came to Jesus could come in the end of the story to possess a faith worthy to be pointed out and praised by Jesus.

Who Touched My Clothes?

When Jesus had felt that power had gone out of him, he turned around to the crowd and said, "Who touched my clothes?" This is another much discussed detail of the story.

Most interpreters think Jesus knew all the time who had touched him. He asked simply to make the woman confess her actions publicly and openly.

Cranfield however represents those who disagree. He states, "He does not know. And he seeks information, not because he wishes to make the miracle conspicuous — which would be inconsistent with his injunctions to secrecy — but because he desires to draw away from his clothes to himself an imperfect faith which was seeking help apart from a personal relationship with himself."[11]

This would seem to be supported by Mark's use of the term "looked round about." It is a word or expression common to Mark. It is even more forceful in the Greek. It presents a suspenseful, dramatic picture of Jesus looking all around, his eyes wandering from one face to another in the crowd, until he saw the one who had done this thing.

It is a term that could appropriately be used to describe a sand-lot captain of a ballgame carefully surveying all the kids standing about, deciding whom he is going to choose to be on his team. It indicates careful, deliberate scrutiny.

Panic

When the eyes of Christ fell on the woman who had just touched him and been healed, she panicked. Suddenly she realized what her cure had cost. She had committed a horrible crime and had been caught in the act. When the crowd discovered what had happened, she would certainly be stoned to death on the spot. Not only had she contaminated them — but their beloved leader as well.

But to her complete surprise Jesus smiles upon her and says, "My daughter, your faith has made you well." Suddenly at this point in the story some amazing realizations move in upon us.

Touching Distance

First, there is the realization that Christ places himself in a position where he can be touched. Here is the self-givingness of God. Here we see the meaning of the Incarnation, that God is with us. God does not dwell in the protective sphere of heaven, inspiring prophets with proclamations and promises, sending messages about his love and concern for us. No! He enters into our lives. As John says, he "tabernacles" with us. He becomes one with us.

Vulnerable

Second, he makes himself vulnerable to us. He opens himself to us so that we, like the woman with the issue of blood, can touch him with our sins and let the contamination which marks our being flow into himself, thereby freeing us from sin and death.

In this story of the woman cured by our Lord, we can see a foretaste of Calvary, where Jesus goes to a cross and opens his body up to take unto himself our sins, working for us a total cure that makes us whole, alive sons and daughters of the living God. The only way we can be cured is for someone to take our infirmities upon himself and suffer for us. This God is not only willing to do — but has done for us.

Sensitivity

Third, we see in this story God's great sensitivity. The Greek words used to describe the setting indicate that Jesus was literally almost suffocated by the crowd. People were pushing in so closely upon him that he could hardly breathe. Yet in the pushing, demanding, shoving mass of humanity, he felt the touch — the touch of one woman in need.

Sometimes when we wonder if God can care for us in such a gigantic universe of pressing needs, when we wonder if our needs are really important to God, we must remember this miracle story. Many people made contact with him that day, but he felt the delicate touch of that one little woman and responded to it.

Sandwich Miracle

The disciples, on the other hand, were not so sensitive. When they heard their master asking, "Who touched me?" the disciples answered, "You see that people are crowding you; why do you ask who touched you?" The tone of the disciples' question indicated they were anxious for Jesus to move on to the important task of curing the daughter of the local synagogue official who was a rich and powerful man.

This miracle is often called a "Sandwich Miracle" because it appears in the center of another miracle. Jairus, a leader of the community and a man with much "clout," had come to throw himself down at the feet of Jesus and beg that his sick daughter might be healed.

The disciples had been pleased and impressed. They had suffered much abuse from their friends for having left all to follow this itinerate preacher who had no respected position either in the religious or social community. Now an important personage of the town had prostrated himself before their leader. The disciples loved it. They couldn't wait to see their Lord and leader cure this important man's daughter. Then they could say to their friends, "See. I told you so. Our Master is also a man of much clout!"

But Jesus paused. He interrupted this important mission to deal with an untouchable woman's needs.

Interruption

The fact that the disciples considered this healing of the woman with the issue of blood a distasteful interruption is understandable. However, they should not have been surprised by it. Again and again during his earthly ministry, Christ was interrupted by human needs, and each time he responded.

Hendriksen is impressed with the fact that none of these intrusions ever floored Jesus so that for the moment he was at a loss what to do or say. What the disciples called an *interruption* became for Jesus "a springboard or take off point for the utterance of a great saying, or, as here, for the performance of a marvelous deed, revealing his power, wisdom, and love."[12]

For our Lord, interruptions were transformed into golden opportunities. Christ looked upon this woman and saw in her superstitious attitude the opportunity to create a great faith.

Tschaikowsky's *Andante Cantabile* is one of the loveliest of his compositions. On a summer vacation, Tschaikowsky heard a Russian baker singing a popular song which began, "Vanya sat on the divan and smoked a pipe of tobacco." That is what this gifted artist started with. He saw the possibilities in the ordinary and miraculously transformed it into this great musical classic, *Andante Cantabile.*

So Christ with his great sensitivity felt the touch of a superstitious woman in need and recognized an opportunity to create within her great faith.

Is our sensitivity sometimes blunted when we are engaged in what we think is really important for the clout of our church in the community, so that we neglect and overlook the big needs of little people, viewing their touch as an interruption? Not so with our Lord. Responding to the request of an important official of the synagogue, he still had the time and the sensitivity to pause and help out this little woman with her big need.

The Whole Truth

Christ responded to the touch of this lady by reaching out and touching her to make her whole.

Chadwick is impressed by the fact that Jesus deals gently with this woman. He comments, "This enfeebled and emaciated woman was allowed to feel in her body that she was healed of her plague, before she was called upon for her confession."[13]

It is important that her confession followed her cure. She did not come to Jesus, as others had, begging for help. She sang no litany as she entered into this encounter with the Lord. She came as a secret sinner. The only thing she brought to Christ was her disease and an unexpressed desire to be well. The decisive issue of this story is therefore not what she *brought* to Jesus but what he *gave* to her.

William Kelly, writing to this point, says, "But even conscious assurance is not enough for the grace of God. She had stolen, as it were, the blessing; she must have it a free and full gift from the Lord, face to face."[14]

This is the gospel. She brings nothing. Christ gives her everything. He not only heals her; he makes her whole.

Three Important Terms

The miracle story ends with Jesus saying to the woman, "My daughter, your faith has made you well! Go in peace, and be healed from your trouble." Three terms concern us in this statement: "My daughter," "your faith," and "Go in peace."

My Daughter

Seldom in the New Testament does Jesus use such a personal form of address. So when he does, we can assume there is a reason for it.

Hendriksen believes that "by means of these cheering words Jesus also opened the way for the woman's complete reinstatement in the social and religious life and fellowship of her people."[15]

This would suggest Jesus used the term "my daughter" for the sake of the bystanders who were looking on. However, when we consider the shock which this woman must have suffered at being publicly exposed, it would seem that our Lord's use of the term was a means of indicating his love and concern for her.

Mark says, "The woman realized what had happened to her; so she came, trembling with fear, and fell at his feet and told him the whole truth." In the light of this traumatic confession, the words of Jesus, "My daughter," were words of absolution spoken to her. By this Jesus was saying, "I forgive you."

This is an exciting insight into the meaning of forgiveness. Often we tend to think of forgiveness as the blotting out of sins, the erasing of past deeds, like taking a cloth and wiping the marks from a chalkboard, or stamping across an account, "Paid in Full."

Forgiveness is that, but it is so much more. It is the re-establishment of a relationship. Jesus says, "My daughter," and by this he indicates to her and to us that forgiveness makes of us true sons and daughters of God our Father.

Some liturgical scholars argue that the act which occurs within the Service of Confession should not be referred to as "Absolution" but "The Declaration of Grace." And this is the point made in our miracle story.

To absolve is to do away with something. Webster defines *absolve* as "to free from penalty," or "release from an obligation."

A "Declaration of Grace," however, is not doing away with something but the *bestowing of something*. It is not a debt canceled, but a gift given. True, forgiveness involves both, but the positive aspect of forgiveness as the gift of a new relationship is frequently neglected or at least underplayed.

When Jesus says to this woman, "My daughter," he is speaking to us. He is saying the same thing he once said to the person who asked him about his mother and his brothers. "Who is my mother? Who are my brothers?" Then Jesus pointed to his disciples saying, "Look! Here are my mother and my brothers! For the person who does what my Father in heaven wants him to do is my brother, my sister, and my mother" (Matthew 12:48, 49).

Thus the first term, "My daughter," leads us to the important fact that, because Christ establishes this new relationship between us and God, we can now have faith.

Your Faith

The phrase "your faith" causes all kinds of trouble for the student of this miracle story. It is frequently used to encourage people to develop by their own sheer force of will power greater faith. "Believe strongly enough and you can accomplish anything you desire." Faith healers shout forth in their meetings, "You can be healed, if only you believe!" However, the text does not assume or justify such faith-formulas of instantaneous healing on the basis of a believer's effort.

Rawlinson expresses the opinion of most scholars when he writes, "The Lord, in any case, does not describe the cure as a case of 'faith-healing' in the modern sense, as though this woman had been cured because she believed she was cured. For him, as for her, the cure is the work of God."[16]

It is helpful in understanding this approach to realize that the term "your faith" should not be taken in the *possessive* sense but in the *locative* sense. Christ with this statement is identifying what had happened *in* her. God had been at work in her.

She had been chosen and confronted by the Father as she stood in the presence of Jesus. God had entered into her and had given her the power of healing, and this act was the act of faith. In this encounter with God the Father, she had been made well. Her faith was not something she brought to Jesus, but it was something God had given her when she came into the presence of Jesus.

We have established the biblical understanding of the word "faith" as *relationship* — a personal relationship with God. Jesus locates this relationship as occurring first within the heart, which means the center and innermost being of a person. For Jesus the heart is like a cup. It is never empty. It is either filled up with the love of self, or the personal presence of the living God, the spirit of God. To possess faith is literally to be possessed by God. To have faith is to have a heart filled to the brim with God's presence and power.

Faith, in the New Testament, is a personal relationship existing between a person and God. It is a God-possessed heart and life that is a gift from God. Faith is not an activity of human effort. It is just the opposite. It is, so far as a person is concerned, a state of human *passivity*, surrendering to a God who desires to possess us and establish a relationship with us. Faith is God's action in us.

Speaking of Jesus' response to this woman, Lenski writes, "When faith is praised highly it is because of the contents of faith."[17] That hits the nail squarely on the head. Faith is to be thought of as the "contents" of our hearts. When God enters in and fills us with himself, then we are people who possess faith.

Go In Peace

Rawlinson, referring to the term "Go in peace," comments, "The phrase is not a mere formula of dismissal, but a word of reassurance that all is well. Henceforward there will be no recurrence of her malady."[18]

Rawlinson is right in his observation that this phrase is more than a formula of dismissal, but he does not say enough. It is so much more than just a reassurance that there will be no recurrence of the disease. The phrase "Go in peace" is a statement of new beginnings. This woman was not being restored to her old life before she contracted the disease which plagued her. She was entering into a new and better life than she had ever known before. She was beginning a life of fellowship with God.

Saint Veronica

The story of this woman has stimulated the imagination of many of the early church fathers. Men like Ambrose, Jerome, Hilary, and others gave her the name of Veronica from Paneas. In the non-canonical *Gospel of Nicodemus* (Chapter 5, verse 26), this woman with the issue of blood is also identified as Veronica.

In the tradition of the church, Saint Veronica is the woman who on the road to Calvary came forth from the crowds that lined the streets and wiped the perspiration from the face of our Lord as he labored under the weight of the cross. Tradition says that when she withdrew the towel, the sweat of Christ had left an indelible image of our Savior's face upon the towel.

Gabriel Max has immortalized this tradition in his fascinating painting of *Veronica's Veil*, copies of which hang in many a pastor's study. With his artistic skill, Max has painted the eyes of Jesus so that at first glance they seem closed, but as one continues to look at the eyes, they open and Christ is staring directly into the observer's eyes.

Even if we have never seen Gabriel Max's painting, a meditative consideration of this miracle story and the tradition of *Veronica's Veil* can conjure up in our imaginations magnificent pictures of our own. The woman who once touched the hem of his garment and came to know the self-giving, sacrificial love, and sensitivity of Christ for her problem, the woman who was healed by this experience and was given a new chance to live again, this woman now mops the bitter perspiration from the brow of that same young man on his way to the cross.

He who had given this woman new life was about to die. And in his dying he was to give her and us an even greater life. He who once stopped the flow of blood from this woman's body in order to heal her, must not now stop the flow of blood from his own body in order to heal us all.

The story of the woman who was healed of an issue of blood is a great miracle. But the greatest miracle of all is the unstopped issue of blood that flowed from the body of God's Son and our Savior as he hung crucified for and by our sins. This miracle alone can heal and give us life today.

141

1. Ronald S. Wallace, *The Gospel Miracles* (Grand Rapids, Michigan: William B. Eerdmans Publishing Company, 1960), p. 81.

2. *Ibid.*, p. 86.

3. William Hendriksen, *Exposition of the Gospel According to Mark*, New Testament Commentary (Grand Rapids, Michigan: Baker Book House, 1975), p. 209.

4. R. C. H. Lenski, *The Gospel Selections of the Ancient Church* (Columbus, Ohio: Lutheran Book Concern, 1936), p. 927.

5. Hendriksen, *op. cit.*, p. 205.

6. William Barclay, *And He Had Compassion* (Valley Forge: Judson Press, 1975), p. 47.

7. Clovis Chappell, *Sermons from the Miracles* (New York: Abingdon-Cokesbury Press, 1937), p. 155.

8. Lenski, *op. cit.*, p. 928.

9. Walter Lowrie, *Jesus According to St. Mark* (New York: Longmans, Green and Company, 1929), p. 189.

10. William L. Lane, *The Gospel According to St. Mark* (Grand Rapids, Michigan: William B. Eerdmans Publishing Company, 1974), p. 193.

11. C. F. B. Cranfield, *The Gospel According to St. Mark* (London: Cambridge University Press, 1959), p. 185.

12. Hendriksen, *op. cit.*, p. 204.

13. G. A. Chadwick, *The Gospel According to St. Mark* (New York: A. C. Armstrong and Son, 1893), p. 155.

14. William Kelley, *An Exposition of the Gospel of Mark* (Pennsylvania: Believers Bookshelf, 1971), p. 75.

15. Hendriksen, *op. cit.*, p. 210.

16. A. E. J. Rawlinson, *St. Mark* (London: Methuen and Company, Ltd., 1942), p. 69.

17. Lenski, *op. cit.*, p. 929.

18. Rawlinson, *op. cit.*, p. 69.

Mark 6:30-44

Proper 11
Pentecost 9
Ordinary Time 16

Miracle 7

The Good Grocer

The Miracle Of The Feeding Of The Multitude

Matthew 14:13-21; 15:32-39; Luke 9:10-17;
John 6:1-13 *(parallel texts)*

Most of us remember from our nursery rhyme days a little old lady by the name of Mother Hubbard. The story went like this:

Old Mother Hubbard
Went to her cupboard
to get her poor dog a bone.
When she got there
the cupboard was bare
and her poor dog had none.

This is really a poem depicting the poverty that constantly plagues humanity. The poverty of bread — the perennial problem of feeding the vast population of our world. We who live in supermarket America where we weekly push carts through crowded aisles surrounded by shelves loaded with abundance often forget that the majority of the people of the world go to bed hungry and wake up in the morning wondering where their next meal is coming from. Our only problem is what kind of bread to buy. Because of this it is easy to overlook the impact the multiplication of bread had on those poor Galileans who first witnessed this miracle.

The average man in the days of our Lord worked for a denarius a day and that was the amount needed to feed his family. Fail to work and you and your loved ones failed to eat that day. There

143

were no unemployment benefits, no credit cards, no food stamps. It was a hand-to-mouth existence. If you did come by some extra food, there was no way to store it up for a rainy day, for there was no refrigerator or handy deep freeze in the kitchen. If the people had a theology, it was concerned, therefore, not so much with grace as with groceries. If God were good, it meant one thing — he provided their daily bread.

This is undoubtedly one of the reasons why the Jewish faith was marked so consistently with meal images. Sacrifice was the offering up to God of scarce and, therefore, sacred food — the roasted lamb and the freshly baked bread. Family worship was a table fellowship of a shared meal. Heaven was a banquet with the Messiah as the host.

The priest talked of ritual cleanliness, and the Pharisees argued the fine points of the Law, and the rabbi reminded the people of the great heritage of their race, but the common, ordinary people looked to God as the giver of groceries — food — daily bread. This was their understanding of religion and the level of their theology.

So when the people heard that Jesus was the Bread of Life, they knew at once that he was their kind of man. And when they heard the story about how he multiplied the bread and fed the multitude, he was their kind of Messiah and they wanted to hear that story over and over again.

This is why the feeding of the multitude was the most popular miracle in the whole New Testament. Every Gospel writer records it once and Matthew and Mark tell it twice. It was not the miracle of the story that made it attractive, but the simple fact that it concerned the most ordinary and yet most important thing in the daily lives of people — bread.

Banking With God

Now as the word "bread" appealed to the hungry first-century Jews, the word "multiplied" appeals to the ambitious and security-minded among us today. In our financially-dominated culture, multiplication is a key concept of our economy and is translated "rate of interest" or "dividend." How much profit does an investment yield?

When we are children we first learn to add — two plus two equals four. Then we learn to subtract and finally we advance to the stage of multiplication. At this stage we begin to learn what life is all about. We are no longer satisfied with getting things to add up; we want them to multiply. We are no longer satisfied with placing three apples on a table, taking away one and having two apples left. Now we figure out how to invest in an apple orchard and make a few apples produce an abundant harvest and enormous profits.

A person who hides his money in a tin can and buries it in the backyard is an eccentric old fool. Now we invest our money in a government-guaranteed bank where it will draw the maximum interest and multiply. This means success and security. So it is in all areas of life. We want our personal possessions to multiply — not just to add up, but to multiply.

So when we read this miracle of the feeding of the multitude it sounds good. Rely on the Lord and the power of God will multiply the loaves and the fishes of our lives. In the long run, God and God alone pays the highest rate of interest on the investments of our time, our talents, and of life itself. So invest in him and success and security will be ours. But is this the message of the miracle? Let us see.

The Popular Jesus

Ronald Wallace[1] makes much of the fact that this miracle occurs at the heights of Jesus' popularity. Expectations were running high. The crowds thronged about Jesus wanting to hear about the Kingdom of God and all the good things which were to come. They wanted their sick healed and their broken spirits lifted. The crowds always make demands of their popular heroes. And when the long, hard day came to an end, they looked to Jesus to be fed.

Wallace believes the practical issue here is, could Jesus deal with the demands and problems raised by his own sheer popularity? It is obvious that the disciples could not. They were embarrassed and helpless and said, "Send them away."

Wallace then adds that popularity often embarrasses and frightens the church. When faced with the vast responsibilities of dealing with the whole community, today's distressed disciples want to cry out, "Send them away." We cannot meet all the demands made upon the church. "Charity begins at home," we think. It is impossible for us to feed the world and support missions and evangelism in every dark corner of the earth. But, Wallace points out, we must remember the thrust of this miracle of the feeding assures us that when Christ is in our midst, "The church is always adequate for the emergency or crisis in the affairs of his people."[2]

A Tired Jesus

The popularity of Jesus did, however, take a great deal of his energy. He was every inch a man and he got tired just as we do. When our story opens he is seeking a place to rest. He was not only physically tired; he was mentally exhausted. He had just heard of the death of his cousin, John the Baptizer. It was a great personal shock and he undoubtedly saw, even in this moment of popularity, the shadow of the cross falling across his path. He sensed in a special way that John's death foreshadowed his own.

Mark points out that the seventy had just reported back — mission accomplished. The time seemed right for a much-needed vacation for them all. So he got into a boat with the disciples and headed for "a lonely place apart."

Then a touch of pathetic humor enters the story. When Jesus and his disciples arrived at their vacation spot, they discovered the crowd had circled the lake on foot, had arrived ahead of them, and were waiting eagerly for a full day's activity of teaching and healing. It would be like a weary pastor taking a day off to go to the beach with his family only to discover the young people of his church had decided to hold a beach picnic at the very same spot he had chosen to relax.

Here in our story we see a miracle almost as great as the multiplication of the bread. Tired, exhausted, tense over the thoughts of his coming death, he was not annoyed at the demanding crowd, but had compassion on them and actually welcomed the opportunity of teaching the people and healing their sick. As the day wore on and our Lord was wearing out, the setting sun indicated the meeting should come to an end. Now our Lord was faced with the task of feeding the people. They had received the bread of his words;

146

now they needed bread for their physical hunger. It was a big task, for they were a big crowd.

Many

The number 5,000, or 4,000 according to one account, should not be taken as a mathematical count. Such precise head-counting is not typical of the Hebrew mind. They were not concerned with statistics. Rather, it should be taken as a dramatic expression meaning "many people were there." When they did count people, only men were counted, which would mean that if you did want an exact figure, it would have to be doubled or even tripled when considering the women and children who must have been present. Knowing the population of this area, a crowd of ten to fifteen thousand seems to be extremely unlikely. Therefore, the figure 5,000 or 4,000 should not be pushed. Simply accept what the Gospel writers meant by using these figures. They meant that many people were present.

When Jesus remarks, "Some of them have come a long way," this could be explained by the fact that this was the time of the Passover and many in the crowd may have been pilgrims on their way to the Passover Feast at Jerusalem. This could explain the unusual size of the crowd. But it also creates a problem, for pilgrims would have undoubtedly brought along sufficient food for their journey. The role of the little boy in the story might shed some light on this.

Philip, Andrew, And A Little Boy

Then Jesus suggests to the disciples that the people should be fed. John has Jesus turning to Philip and asking of him, "Where can we buy enough food to feed all these people?" Philip was a local boy; he had come from Bethsaida (John 1:44) so it was only natural that Jesus would turn to him, for if anyone knew the local situation Philip would. But Philip isn't much help; he is more concerned with the fact that they have little or no money. Among them all the disciples had only a denarius which was an average day's wage. And Philip points out that it would take at least six months' wages to feed this mob.

147

Then Andrew, Simon Peter's brother, speaks up, "There is a boy here who has five loaves of barley bread and two pickled salt-fish." When the other disciples heard Andrew report, they must have had a good laugh. Five loaves of barley bread and two salt-fish would not provide a picnic for a small family, let alone this huge crowd of hungry guests waiting to be fed. But Jesus did not laugh. He willingly took this lunch box belonging to a little boy and he made of it a catering service that satisfied the needs of a crowd.

Miracle Of Generosity

Some scholars have suggested that the actions of the boy shamed the crowd into sharing what they had been holding back for themselves. Many in the crowd, knowing that they would be away from home all day, had brought food for their own needs. But when they noticed that some brought nothing they were unwilling to produce their lunches for the simple reason that they did not wish to share it with others. Then there were the pilgrims in the crowd. They certainly had supplies along with them. But they had a trip ahead of them and they needed all the food they had for their journey.

The action of the little boy touched them and shamed them and they opened their picnic baskets and shared what they had with those around them. When the available resources were thus pooled, there was enough food for all. Barclay states, "If we take it that way, this would be a miracle where the influence of Jesus changed the crowd of selfish people to a crowd of people willing to share what they had."[3]

This, of course, dismisses the idea that this was a nature miracle where the loaves are multiplied and establishes it as an event of Christ's influential power over people. The conclusion would be that Christ brings out the best in people. This is true, but it hardly seems to do justice to the fact that this story was important enough for it to find a place in all four of the Gospels.

Actually this interpretation would seem to suggest that the main character in the story was the little boy rather than Christ, for it was what he did that changed the people and not the influential power of Christ. Knowing John and his theological interests, he certainly would not give room in his Gospel for a neat little moral story about a small boy who moved a crowd of people to be generous. This event had greater significance than such a simple interpretation would suggest.

Organization

After Jesus had the meager contribution of the lad's lunch, he turned to the disciples and gave them directions: "Make the people sit down." The people, the story recounts, sat down in sections. The word used here [*Prasiai*] is normally used for rows of vegetables in a garden. The picture is made quite clear by the writer. The vast number of people ceased to be a chaotic crowd and became an organized congregation.

This would suggest the importance of organization in the work of the Kingdom. If we are to accomplish anything positive in the process of establishing the Kingdom of God in the world, there is a need for an organization — an administrative structure. Sometimes it is difficult to appreciate the vast machinery of the church. It seems contrary to the breath of the spirit that moves in the realm of faith. But when faith takes on the dimensions of the world, efficient organization becomes necessary if we are to work effectively in our contemporary culture. There is a vast difference between a picnic lunch for the family and feeding a multitude of people.

So the people were gathered into well-ordered groups and sat down on the "green grass." This detail would suggest that the feeding took place in the spring of the year.

Table Grace

Then Jesus took the bread and looked up to heaven. Sometimes it is assumed that Jesus blessed the bread, which suggests a sacramental aspect of the miracle. Now the sacrament may be implied here by the author, but it should be noted that Jesus does not bless the bread; rather, he gave thanks to God. More than likely he used the common prayer of Jewish family life:

Blessed art thou
O, Lord our God
King of the world
who has brought forth
bread from the earth.

There is a Jewish saying, "He who enjoys anything without thanksgiving is as though he robbed God." The fact that Jesus looked up to heaven and gave thanks could mean that the intention of what he did when he fed the multitude was simply to get them to see that all good things come from God. He wanted the people to see not bread multiplied, but God *glorified*. As he had taught the multitude with words, now he was teaching them with actions. As he fed them, he was teaching the people that beyond the bread was the God who provides all bread and provides it abundantly.

But the crowds that day, much like us today, were blinded by bread and abundance. That's all they saw, a miracle of multiplied bread. They left convinced that Jesus was a great Bread Messiah. They wanted to hear more from this fabulous fellow who was able to more than adequately supply and satisfy all their needs. This is just what they have been looking for — a leader with great power potential. If anyone could solve their needs, this Jesus appeared to be the hottest prospect in all Judea.

They Left A Tip

Each account agrees that the crowd had as much as they could eat and when every person was full, Jesus said to his disciples, "Pick up the pieces left over; let us not waste a bit." The leftovers are frequently translated as "fragments." The Greek word [*Peah*] used here is suggestive. It refers to the fragments left over at a social banquet. It was the food for the servants who had attended the guests. It was very much like what today we call tips. Our word for tip comes from an old English custom where a small box was placed in eating establishments. Printed on the box were the letters T-I-P, which stood for, "To Insure Promptness." So the guests at this lakeside party politely left tips for the disciples — twelve baskets full, one basket for each of the disciples.

Allegorical Interpretation

Many approaches have been made in an attempt to make this scriptural passage preachable in all times. The earliest interpretation was allegorical.

Ever since the time of Augustine the feeding of the 5,000 has been taken as a sign of Jesus' self-communication to the Jews, and the feeding of the 4,000 has been a sign to the Gentiles.

One basis for this is that Mark uses two different words for "basket" in his two accounts of the story. In the feeding of the 5,000, he uses *kophinos*, which describes the food basket the Jews carried to insure they would have ceremonially clean food when they were away from home. It was a jug-like basket, narrow at the top and wide at the bottom. In the feeding of the 4,000, he uses *sphuris*, which describes a type of basket used by the Gentiles. It was shaped like a hamper.

The allegorical approach has its adherents up to this day. Scholars like Alan Richardson, Vincent Taylor, and John Sunduall point out that the feeding of the 5,000 is located on the western side of the lake of Galilee in Jewish territory, whereas the feeding of the 4,000 is placed in Gentile territory on the eastern side of the lake.

Other facts are also given to support an allegorical approach. The number of people — 5,000 — and the five loaves of bread refer to the five books of the Jewish *Torah*. The twelve baskets which are taken up represent the twelve tribes of Israel and therefore suggest a Jewish audience. On the other hand, in the account of the 4,000 the number seven takes the place of the five and the twelve. The people receive seven loaves which would be understood as a reference to the seventy nations into which the Gentile world was traditionally divided.

Voobus, however, categorically denies the validity of the allegorical approach. He states, "The scrutiny of the facts shows that in the evangelist's mind no such allegory was involved when he wrote the narratives."[4] And the balance of modern scholarship would tend to agree. Particularly is this true of those who view the feeding of the 4,000 and the 5,000 as a doublet, a twice-told story.

Most interpretations of this miracle can be placed in two categories: those that look backward and those that look forward.

151

The Backward-Looking Interpretation
Scholars find in this story a considerable resemblance to certain Old Testament narratives. Two of the Hebrews' great heroes, Elisha and Moses, had been providers of miraculous bread.

The Lord Of Plenty
When Elisha came to Gilgal (2 Kings 4:38) there was a great famine in the land and he took a few loaves of barley bread and ears of corn and fed the people.

When the children of God were in the wilderness they murmured to God and against Moses because they were dying of hunger. They even wished to be back in slavery where they could at least eat. Then God spoke to Moses, and manna from heaven was provided to fill their empty stomachs.

The feeding of the multitude, therefore, appears as an antitype pointing back to the feeding of Israel in the biblical past, with one great difference. Whereas Elisha and Moses provided food only to meet the needs, Jesus provided an abundance, more than enough. Therefore, a greater one than Elisha and Moses has come. Jesus is not only the prophet who provides bread; he is the Lord who provides plenty!

Forward-Looking Interpretations
Many scholars, when interpreting this miracle, look forward rather than backward and, it should be noted, a few look both ways. When they look forward, they see the event of the miracle pointing toward the future toward events which are to happen.

Some see in it a prefigurement of the Eucharist. The terminology — "he took, he blessed, he brake, he gave" — suggests the four-fold action of the Eucharist so firmly established by the great liturgical scholar, Gregory Dix.

Alan Richardson picks up on the phrase "having given thanks" and points out that this literally means "having made eucharist." Richardson continues, "The lakeside meal is a foreshadowing of the church's Eucharist and of the feast of the redeemed in the Kingdom of God."[5] A. M. Hunter goes so far as to say that this event is "the Galilean Lord's Supper."

Voobus finds great difficulty with this interpretation. He sees no mention of forgiveness in the account and he points out, "The Eucharist does not mean just free admission for everyone, but that personal repentance is as necessary as belief that Jesus is the Christ." Neither repentance nor belief in Christ is mentioned in the account and, therefore, the early church could not have seen in this event a connection to their Eucharist.

It is also true that there is no evidence in the story that the group fed was a community of the faithful. The Eucharist at the time this event was recorded was a closed cultic act. It was limited strictly to baptized believers. A public picnic could hardly symbolize such a carefully guaranteed experience.

However, supporting the Eucharistic theory are the hard facts of archaeology. In the Catacombs and in much Christian art of the early centuries, the symbol of the loaves and the fishes is commonly accepted as referring to the Eucharist. For example, in the Catacomb of Calixtus in the sacrament chapel, a fish is shown with a basket of bread resting upon his back. In the funeral meal chamber in the Catacomb of Priscilla, there are seven baskets of bread placed in front of the communion table. There can be little doubt that this is an allusion to John 6.[6]

The most acceptable approach to this interpretation comes from Van der Loos. He states:

> *Establishing a connection between the miraculous feeding and the sacrament of Holy Communion doubtless has great significance from the theological point of view, provided that it is borne clearly in mind that the connection is not present in an immediate, historical sense. The text merely says that the physical hunger of the people was the issue ... As in the healings, it is obvious in the feeding that the saving love of Jesus Christ relates to man in his totality.*[7]

What Van der Loos is saying here is that Jesus Christ is the Bread of Life and provides for the total needs of people. In the past God fed his people manna in the wilderness. That day by the side of a lake God in Christ fed the people bread to fulfill their hunger. At

153

the table of Holy Communion God feeds us with the words of forgiveness and the assurance that we are one with him. In the future we shall all rejoice at the table of the Lord when we are privileged to partake of the great Messianic Banquet. The one common thread which runs throughout is Christ, the Bread of Life, "he who provides for all our needs."

Eschatology

As we have pointed out, some scholars who look forward when interpreting this miracle take an eschatological view of the feeding of the multitude. It is seen as a pledge and a foretaste of the celestial banquet in God's eternal Kingdom.

Even though Albert Schweitzer cannot accept this story of the feeding as a miracle, he does believe that the event actually happened. He writes, "All of this is historical but not the final remark that they were all filled. Jesus caused the food which he and his disciples had with them to be distributed among the people, so that everyone received a piece." Jesus is the coming Messiah and therefore he performs a sacramental act which is the antitype of the great Messianic Feast of the future. Schweitzer makes it quite clear that he is not talking about our current Eucharist. He goes on to say, "The feeding was more than a love feast, a communal meal. It was, from Jesus' point of view, a sacrament of salvation."[8] This event was the anticipative epiphany of the Messiah, a foretaste of the future Messianic meal at the end of time.

Two Kinds Of Bread

When a survey is made of the many sermons preached on this text, it is obvious that the generosity of the boy that moved a selfish crowd to share what they had is a popular interpretation of this miracle. The idea that Jesus is concerned for the total person is also a frequently chosen theme. Luther, for example, points out that our Lord provides "the soul with the Word of God and the body with bread."

Theodore Parker Ferris[9] has a sermon where he deals with two kinds of bread. There is the ordinary bread, the kind we eat. This is the bread we put on our tables and it includes the meat and potatoes, vegetables and sweets. This is the bread we live *on*.

Then there is another kind of bread. We don't eat it; we experience it, see it, feel it, think it, dream it, and imagine it. We devour it with the mysterious equipment of our being. It takes existence and makes of it a life worth living. This is the bread we live *by*. For example, when children go to school they take their lunch boxes filled with peanut butter sandwiches and an apple, a bottle of milk. This is the food they live on.

But they also need the love and affection of their parents, the interest of their teachers, the attention and the acceptance of their friends. They need the joy of play, the excitement of new ideas, the thrill of adventure, and even sometimes they need the experience of a good fight. This is the bread they live by.

Now our Lord knows we need both kinds of bread and he is concerned that they be provided for us in abundance. As the Bread of Life he feeds the total person. His message to us in this miracle is: "I have come that you might have life" — both kinds of bread — "and have it more abundantly."

Spotlight On The Disciples

In all six accounts, the disciples play a decisive role. They do not play the lead; Christ does. As in every miracle story, he is the greatest miracle of all. But the disciples play an important role in the story. It is they who bring the situation to the attention of Jesus. They survey the crowd to see how much food there is. They also get the people to sit down in organized groups so they can be fed. They distribute the bread and gather up the fragments that are left over.

It is true that if the feast on the grass that day would have been left completely to the disciples it would never have come off. Their solution was to send the people away and let them find something to eat for themselves in the nearby farms and villages. But once Jesus took over, the disciples became willing helpers.

The disciples actively participated in the feeding miracle. They were not only among those fed, but they helped others to be fed. They willingly submitted to kitchen work in the Kingdom of God and that says a great deal about their loyalty to their master and Lord.

This also says something directly to us as modern day disciples of the Lord. So often when we hear this miracle we tend to identify ourselves with the ones who were fed. But this is the wrong end of the miracle for us. Rather than at the receiving end, we, as part of the body of Christ, are on the performing end of this miracle.

As we pointed out above, God is concerned for the total needs of people. When we pray, "Give us this day our daily bread," what we mean is, "Please give us everything we need today to live." This means that this miracle should lead us to see the spiritual dimension of the common bread which is farmed and milled, baked, sliced and packaged, delivered and made possible by human sweat and toil. This bread is holy. And the need for bread to feed the hungry of our world is no longer insignificant or secondary. Meeting the needs of people is not an auxiliary function of the church considered only after man's so-called "soul" has been saved. It is, rather, a vital part of the total act of redeeming people.

As we face the feeding of the multitude, we are not just asked to believe that a certain miracle happened 2,000 years ago, but we are called to become involved in a miracle-sized job today. It is the job of feeding the multitude of hungry people in the world now — not just those hungry for food, but for love, forgiveness, peace, and hope — but people who are hungry for a purpose for their lives, companionship in their lonely rooms, hungry for education and beauty. It is God's will that all be fed and fed abundantly, and we are placed on the performing end of this miracle-sized task.

This does not mean we are not to be recipients of God's good work. We are! God gives and we receive far more than we deserve. As a part of all humanity, we are on the receiving end. But as people of faith, disciples of the Bread of Life, the Body of Christ in this world, we are called out of a receiving world to serve the world. We are called to be disciples who carry trays — distribute the gifts of God's grace to others.

This does not imply the trite theology, "God has no hands but our hands," as if God is limited and his gifts are conditional, depending upon the achievement of human effort. No! The Kingdom

156

of God is God at work in the world bringing to pass what he wills. And this he can accomplish with or without us. But the glorious good news of it all is that God has invited us to become involved with him, to become participants in his continual redemptive action whereby he brings all things to his desired end.

On my way home from class I passed the house of one of our married students. He was in the process of raking leaves in his backyard. As I passed I saw him coming around the house carrying a big bundle of leaves to put them in the street in front of his house where they might be picked up by the city. As he rounded the corner of the house, behind him came his three-year-old son holding, in his tight little fist, three or four leaves. His expression indicated the importance of his task in his own mind. He was helping his father.

The importance of this little boy's labor in the total task of transferring leaves from the back to the front of the house was insignificant. But for his personal growth and maturity that little labor was extremely vital. He had the pleasure of being part of the process. He was helping his father.

So we are to carry trays, not for God, or because we are significantly bringing in the Kingdom of God, but for our own sake and for the sake of the many hungry people who will benefit because of our involvement in God's redemptive work. Our calling to carry trays is a privilege of catching a vision of God's will for his world and an opportunity to participate in God's work of feeding the hunger of his children.

Conclusion
We began the study of this miracle with the idea that when we invest our time and talents and life itself in God they will multiply and pay great dividends. Nothing we have learned in our study of this text would deny this fact. However, an important aspect has been added. We are to see ourselves in the light of this miracle not just on the receiving end, but on the giving end.

When we hear this miracle story, we should not stand with our mouths open and our hands extended, waiting to be fed. Rather, God says to us, "I am the Bread of Life. You have been fed and you will be fed, but now I want you to take these trays and help me serve others. As I came as a servant to this world, so I send you forth as the father has sent me — as servants." Take your trays; the evening is coming on and there is a hungry crowd gathering, waiting to be fed their daily bread. God is the good grocer and we are to be his willing servant-clerks.

1. Ronald S. Wallace, *The Gospel Miracles* (Grand Rapids, Michigan: William B. Eerdmans Publishing Company, 1960), p. 88.

2. *Ibid.*, p. 93

3. William Barclay, *And He Had Compassion* (Valley Forge: Judson Press, 1967), p. 149.

4. Arthur Voobus, *The Gospels in Study and Preaching* (Philadelphia: Fortress Press, 1966), p. 214.

5. Alan Richardson, The *Gospel According to John* Torch Commentaries, (London: SCM Press Ltd., 1952), p. 99.

6. F. Van der Meer, *Atlas of the Early Christian World* (London: Thomas Nelson and Sons, Ltd., 1958), p. 42.

7. H. Van der Loos, *The Miracles of Jesus* (Leiden: E. J. Brill, 1968), p. 635.

8. *Ibid.*, p. 628.

9. Theodore Parker Ferris, "The Bread of Life," a sermon preached in Trinity Church, Boston, The Seventh Sunday after Trinity, 1965.

Miracle 8

An Exile Of Silence Set Free

The Healing Of The Deaf Mute

This story is about a man who stumbled into the Kingdom of God without knowing where he was going or why. He was a man forced to live in the non-exotic exile from society called *deafness*. It is strange that blindness receives sympathy in our world, but deafness is considered, as Barclay says, "a nuisance."[1] Yet those who know assure us that nothing cuts a person off from his surroundings as thoroughly as does deafness.

The doctors presented to Beethoven the most crushing blow any musician can encounter. They said to him, "You will hear always less and never again." Beethoven lived in a world of sound. He surrounded himself and was saturated with sound; then suddenly the irrevocable sentence was given that he would live out the remainder of his life in a world of silence. Interestingly enough, when Beethoven wrote of his calamity, he mentioned the social implications of this verdict of silence:

"My misfortune," he wrote, "is doubly painful because it must lead to my being misunderstood, for me there can be no more recreation in the society of my fellows, refined intercourse, mutual exchange of thought, only just as little as the greatest needs command may I mix with society, I must live like an exile."[2]

An exile of silence. This is the tragic state of the man in our miracle story.

The Liturgy Of Hearing

Scholars give various reasons why Mark alone records this story. But for our study this does not concern us as much as the fact that this miracle of healing a deaf man made such a vivid impression on the mind of the early church and imposed itself upon the liturgical practices of the church at an early stage in tradition.

Philip Carrington, speaking of this miracle, informs us that "it is read in the Greek liturgy during the season of Lent when candidates were being prepared for baptism. In Rome it passed into the baptismal ritual and was enacted with the candidates at the same season in the ritual called The Opening of Ears."[3]

Apparently the early church felt that the power of Jesus and his gospel could not express itself adequately in mere words. There was a need for gestures and physical contact. Much as we today are not satisfied just to see or hear a distinguished visitor; we want to shake hands with him if we can. There is a personal value to the sense of physical touch as well as the sense of hearing. The early church caught an almost sacramental quality to this story. It dramatized for them what happens when a person is baptized and given the gift of the Holy Spirit — deaf ears are opened and the baptized person can now hear the living Lord speaking to his people through the words of witness both in the Holy Scriptures and in the personal exchange of testimony within the holy fellowship. Therefore, the church at an early date associated this miracle of the healing of the deaf man with their sacrament of baptism.

Plot-Parallelism

It is interesting to see the comparative similarities of these two stories. The plots are parallel. In the healing of the deaf man the basic plot is: (1) Friends bring the deaf man to Jesus. (2) Jesus takes the man aside. (3) Jesus touches his ears and then his tongue with spittle. (4) Jesus speaks the words, "Be opened!" (5) The deaf man's ears are opened and he speaks.

The parallel plot in the act of baptism is: (1) The parents bring the child to the font. (2) The pastor as the representative of Christ takes the child in his arms. (3) The pastor touches the child with the water of the font. (4) The words are spoken, "In the name of the Father and of the Son and of the Holy Spirit." (5) The sponsors are admonished to teach these newly opened ears the Word of God — the Ten Commandments, the Lord's Prayer, and so on.

In the single plot of these two stories the central truth of the gospel is dramatized. Faith is the response to God's saving act, not the condition of it. Both the deaf mute and the child are brought helpless to the Lord. They do nothing to merit the miracle they receive.

The deaf man's ears were opened, not because he decided no longer to be deaf and chose to hear instead. Rather, Christ chose to open his ears. So we are not baptized because we decide to believe in Christ; we believe because Christ chooses to bring us into the Kingdom of God. We believe because we hear and we hear because the Holy Spirit first opens our ears to the meaning and truth of God's Word.

The deaf man was brought to Jesus. He didn't know where he was going or why. So we do not choose to be born into a Christian family. Nor do we convince our parents to take us to the font. All this happens before we know what is happening. When we come to consciousness we are already admitted into the sphere of Christ's redemption.

In both story plots, God's election remains a mystery. Why this deaf man among all the other deaf people in the district of Decapolis should have been chosen and healed is a mystery. Why we were born into a Christian family and had the advantage of knowing Christ as we were growing to adulthood is a mystery. All we know is that he has chosen us. This idea which is the heart of the apostolic faith is both mystery and miracle. And it is perfectly symbolized in the account of the healing of the deaf mute. Here, as in our baptism, the important thing that happens is what God does, not what we do. Here is the triumph of divine grace which we can never understand, only recognize and celebrate. The only possible reaction to such a free and unmerited gift is to see it as a gift with responsibility. We have not been chosen just to hear; we have been chosen also to speak. Our gift carries with it a responsibility. Given the gift of hearing as the deaf mute, we speak and the words are clear testimony to our Lord — the giver of such good and free grace.

The Speaking God

There may be an even more profound insight into the early church's attraction to this miracle. Greek cultures and thought had always emphasized sight. "Seeing is believing," we still say today, influenced by the scientific mind set of the Greeks. But for the Hebrew culture and thought, the key word was "hear." To hear was to know and obey. An ancient rabbi once remarked that God gave lids to close our eyes but none to close our ears. And he concluded from this, "So God intends that we come to obedience through the hearing of his Word." It was the Word of God that created, directed, and redeemed. The Word was the first line of communication between God and man and the basic source of power and life.

The early church could have so easily seen in this miracle of the healing of the deaf man the heart of their faith — the uniqueness of their God — the speaking God.

Unstopped Ears

Alan Richardson takes this approach toward the miracle and sees it as "St. Mark's desire to symbolize the gradual process of the unstopping of the disciples ears ... The story is for him a parable of the awakening in the disciples' hearts of faith in Jesus' Messiahship."[4]

Wallace follows the same line in his interpretation. He sees this story as a sign. Jesus is saddened by the stupidity of the disciples. They have ears and will not hear. And, he adds, Jesus is still distressed with the church today which lacks understanding of God's Word because it will not listen and learn.

Wallace goes on to say that, immediately after this miracle of the deaf man given his hearing and the miracle of the blind man receiving his sight, "The disciples began to be able to hear and see and to believe the hidden testimony that Jesus was giving to himself in his teachings and miracles." And, Wallace says, "Both these stories are a warning to us about the trouble we ourselves need to take, and the patience and love we may need to exert, in trying to make other people see what we see in Jesus and hear what we hear in his Word."[5]

So the miracle of the healing of the deaf man is a dramatization of the gift of hearing which the Holy Spirit brings to us. We are exiles of silence until God works the miracle and opens our ears to his Word.

Mark begins this story, "Some people brought him a man who was deaf and could hardly speak." Sometimes he is called a deaf-mute but more frequently he is referred to as "deaf and dumb." This has cruel implications to our ears, as we interpret "dumb" to mean ignorant or stupid, and of course this is not the original intent of the word at all. Deaf and dumb simply means a person who cannot speak because he does not hear.

Ear Gate

A young couple was blessed with their first child. He looked perfectly normal and healthy, but gradually they began to notice that he was unresponsive. He seemed to exist in his own little world — unconcerned with what was happening about him. Long after he should have uttered his first sounds he was silent. The parents feared that he was retarded, so they took him to a specialist. After careful examination, the doctor gave his diagnosis. "There is nothing mentally wrong with this child," he said, "except that he is deaf. He does not speak because he has never heard."

What we say and how we say it depends on what we have heard. We cannot produce a sound we have never heard. We have foreign accents, Southern drawls, and New York brogues because that is the way we have heard words pronounced. As a professor of speech graphically expressed it, "What comes out of the door of our mouth, must first come in the gate of our ears."

Today more than at any other time in history we live in a world of sound. Communication media from the telephone to the television flood our ears with sounds, so much so that we develop a noise-deafness. We arrive at a point where we can't tolerate silence. We get up in the morning and the first thing we do, out of sheer habit, is turn on the radio or television. We invest in expensive stereo equipment that literally surrounds us with sound. The result of this "noise-deafness" is that we hear so much, we hear nothing. We have learned to tune out sounds and close the gate of our ears.

163

In this day of liberation and freedom, everyone wants to talk and express opinions; but the problem is that few are willing to listen. And this is where the whole process breaks down. Where there is no prodigious input, there can be no profitable output. We hear a great deal about dialogue today. Many believe the magic solution to all our problems is just to get people together and talk things over. But most dialogues become only a mutual sharing of ignorance. People talk but they don't say anything, and it doesn't really matter because no one is listening. In a dialogue we don't listen to each other because we are too busy thinking about what we are going to say when there is a break in the conversation and we will have a chance to speak.

Now this is a warning for us, because we take our stand theologically on the efficacy of the Word. Our God is a speaking God and we are created, directed, and redeemed by the Word. It follows that the Christian is therefore first and before all else a listener. But in this day of noise-deafness, we no longer know how to listen. Listening is a lost art and we are a deaf people. Our ears need to be opened or we will be condemned to live in the chaos and confusion, the despair and the desperation of deafness. Therefore, our miracle story about Christ healing the deaf-mute has something vital to say to us all.

Do It My Way

The people who brought the deaf man begged Jesus "to place his hand on him." They had seen him heal in this way before. There is little doubt that they meant well. But it is interesting to note that Jesus does not do what they suggest. He will heal the man, but he will do it his own way.

Hendriksen points out, "In dealing with people the Lord chooses his own methods. Naaman had to learn this lesson (2 Kings 5:1-14). So did Jacob, much earlier (Genesis 42:36; 45:25-28). So did also Joseph and his brothers (Genesis 50:15-21). And so, later, did Paul (2 Corinthians 12:7-10). We should never try to tell God what methods he should use in answering our petitions ... just where he should place his hand. His own way is always best."[6]

164

This is typical of the way so many of us come to God. We come not only with a request, but with a preconceived notion of how the request is to be met. We not only ask the Lord for something, but we tell him how we want it done. And when he doesn't fulfill our request to the letter — exactly as we asked him to — we feel he has failed to respond.

A young heiress lived a sensational and glamorous life. New York, Paris, Rome, the Riviera were her playgrounds. She lived high and fast, but her life was empty, shallow, and meaningless.

Then one day she noticed a shadow seemed to pass over her vision. The doctors told her that it may be serious and that tests should be taken. Shocked and desperate, she turned to God seriously for the first time in her life and prayed that her life not be ruined by blindness. The tests were positive and her prognosis was eventual and certain blindness. She was bitter. Her newly-born faith in God was instantly shattered. She turned to her old life, but the attitude of her friends had changed. They were condescending and over-solicitous. She could not endure being pitied.

She decided to run away and hide, like an animal retreating into a cave to die. For years she had financially supported work among the poor of Appalachia. So she decided to spend the last few years of sight among these unfortunates and share their desperation. Within a few months she became involved with these simple but lovable people. She started a much-needed school and discovered for the first time in her life what it meant to be honestly loved and accepted. She found what she had so long searched for — happiness and meaningfulness.

Two years passed and then one morning she awoke and opened her eyes, but there was only darkness. It had happened. She sat for a moment stunned. Then she heard the children on their way to her school. They were laughing and singing. A great calm came upon her. In her diary she records, "As I felt my way along to the classroom, I paused in the garden at the gate. I thought to myself — this gate moves both ways and so with my eyes open or closed I can still teach these children. Then I prayed, 'Thank you, Lord, for taking away my eyes, that my soul might see.' "

Truly God had answered her prayer. She had asked him not to ruin her life with blindness. And God had given her a new and better life, not sparing her from blindness but opening up her whole being to a new and more meaningful style of life.

So God grants our requests, not always as we direct, or the way in which we think they should be answered. He does it his way.

The people begged Jesus to place his hands on the deaf man, but Christ had a better way.

Steps Of The Cure

The steps Jesus takes in the curing of the deaf man are most significant. First he takes him away from the crowd.

The interpretations of this action by scholars are many and varied. Some assert Jesus took the man aside to keep the process of healing secret from the unauthorized. Some simply say that he wanted to avoid publicity. The cross was drawing nearer and Jesus was placing more and more emphasis on the redemptive aspects of his mission. He had come into the world not to be a miracle worker, but the "Savior." He wanted to play down his miracles, for as Hendriksen points out, "The day of the crucifixion must not be hastened."[7] And his miracles more than his messages were pushing his enemies to the final showdown with this troublemaker.

Van der Loos concludes, "We can only say Jesus followed the method that he considered the correct one in certain circumstances and having regard to the persons involved."[8] Barclay is influenced by the fact that deaf people are easily embarrassed and confused. In a crowd they become flustered, excited, and bewildered. Therefore, Jesus calls the deaf man apart from the crowd because of his great sensitivity to the need of people. They need not only to be cured, but to be cured with kindness. Barclay goes so far as to say, "There is no incident in all Jesus' life which so shows his tenderness and consideration for others."[9]

Not denying any of these interpretations, it would seem that there was the practical necessity of getting the man into a position where his complete attention could be placed on Jesus with as few distractions as possible.

The first requirement in learning to listen is *attention*. Much of our lack of hearing is due to distracted attention. We often, for example, find it difficult to remember a person's name we have just met. Because only a few moments have passed since the introduction, our problem is not memory but the fact that we never heard the name in the first place because we were not paying attention. Our minds were elsewhere when the name was mentioned. So attention is vital if our ears are to be opened.

How often the Word of God falls on deaf ears in services of worship because of a misbehaving child or a crying baby, or a fire engine or a plane passes, or the person next to you fiddles with his bulletin, or a choir member falls asleep, or the person behind you strikes up what he alone considers a whispered conversation. Though unintentional, these distractions literally excommunicate listeners from the Word of God. What Luther gave so much of his life to accomplish — namely bringing the Word of God to people — can be destroyed for the moment by the continual crying of a child. There is nothing magical about the Word. It does not work automatically because we are physically present when it is proclaimed. The efficacy of the Word depends upon our hearing that Word and concentrating our attention on that Word. So Jesus called the man apart from the thoughtless crowd that could have unintentionally distracted his attention.

Enters His World And Language System

Jesus has taken the deaf man aside and now enters into his world. He uses the deaf man's language system to communicate with him. They are alone. Positioned before Jesus, the man's eyes make contact with this strange young man who apparently wants to help him. Each move Jesus makes is meaningful to him.

The second step of the cure is that Jesus places his fingers into the deaf man's ears. This touch of Jesus should not be interpreted in the sense of a power transfer. And, as Van der Loos warns us, "Nor must we seek to establish a resemblance between touching by Jesus and so-called 'tactile stimuli' as employed by present-day suggestive therapy."[10]

Rather, the placing of his fingers in the deaf man's ears is simple sign language to indicate that he knows where the man's problem lies. The same is true of Jesus' touching the man's tongue. As Lenski says, "Jesus fastened the deaf-mute's full attention upon his two great disabilities."[11] Jesus literally puts his finger on the problem.

At the same time, Jesus' touch linked and related him to the sick person as it did when he touched the leper, the blind man, and Peter's mother-in-law. Jesus communicated his love as well as his diagnosis of the situation. Both problem and person are dealt with. By his touch, Jesus not only indicates he knows what is wrong, but he wants to and will help the man.

Every mother knows what is happening here. For when she holds her newborn child for the first time, he is as yet deaf to the language of the adult world in which he has entered. So she enters into his world and uses his language. She talks with fingertips of love. She communicates with caresses. In her tender embrace and body warmth, the child knows that it is cared for and welcomed into this strange new world. The amazing vocabulary and grammar of gesture, touch, and movement bring two persons together in mutual understanding — a mother and her child relate to each other.

He Spat

The additional note that Jesus "spat" upon his finger before touching the man's tongue brings up the whole issue of the role "spittle" played in cures at the time of Jesus. In the days of our Lord, saliva was "soul power." It was a sign that Jesus was giving himself personally to this man. It was also a sign of medical cures. Swete points out, "Saliva was regarded as remedial, but the custom of applying it with incantation seems to have led the rabbis to denounce its use. Possibly it appealed more strongly than any other symbol that could have been employed."[12]

Power From On High

The third step of the cure is, "Jesus looked up to heaven." This was to indicate the nature of the power that was going to remove the deaf man's disabilities. The power was coming from on high

— from God. From our story we know very little about this man personally. But it is safe to assume that he was a religious man. In the three-level universe in which he lived, this gesture was, therefore, extremely significant.

A Sigh Too Deep For Words

The fourth step: Jesus sighed or "gave a deep groan." It was a sigh too deep for words. Some scholars have seen in this an intense prayer that resembled the desperate cry of the Litany, "Lord, have mercy upon us." Barclay sees not only this but also a groan of sheer compassion for the wretched state of the man.[13]

There is, however, another possible interpretation. The Jews in their religious thought patterns associated the life-giving power of God with the concept of *breath*. In the beginning act of creation (Genesis 2:7) God breathed into man the breath of life. The Psalmist sings, "By the word of the Lord were the heavens made; and all the hosts of them by the breath of his mouth" (Psalm 33:6). And it was the breath of God which gave life to the dry bones in Ezekiel (37:5).

When Jesus gave the great sigh, the deaf man could easily have recalled his teaching in the synagogue and saw in this action that Jesus was drawing the creative and restoring breath of God into himself that would give life to silent ears. It was a sign of strength, strength to destroy silence and restore this man to the world of sound.

Ephphatha

The final step is Jesus speaking the word *Ephphatha*. Jesus has communicated his care and concern. The contact has been made and the deaf mute now stands on the cutting edge of his cure. As the word is spoken the ears are opened. The silence is broken. The man is free.

An Enacted Sermon

Jesus must have shouted these words, "Be opened!" for the crowd nearby heard and rushed to discover that the deaf man's ears had been opened. His tongue was set loose and they heard him speak plainly.

Those people had seen a sermon enacted that day. When Jesus shouted, "Ephphatha — Be opened" and they heard the deaf man speak without defects, they knew that something marvelous had happened and somehow they were involved in it. The healing grace of God proclaimed to one is proclaimed to all. In their minds there was little doubt that God was here announcing and initiating the promised Kingdom for all. Jesus stood before the crowd as the incarnate fulfillment to the prophet's promise that the eyes of the blind would be opened and the ears of the deaf would be unstopped. The ministry of healing to that deaf person was an effective sign, an enacted sermon announcing that in Christ the Kingdom of God had come. In a universe of silence, God had spoken and his word opened the ears of all people to a message of love, forgiveness, hope and a glorious new life.

Stubbornness — Man And God

One thing that is a common cause of deafness to the Word of God is stubbornness. It is a natural expression of our sinful nature. We frequently refer to a person as being "stubborn as a mule," or "bull-headed." I suppose in the animal world, if they could talk, one bull would say to his obstinate bull-friend that he was "human-headed," and you know he would be right. For of all the creatures God created, man has less excuse for this perverse attitude called "stubbornness." God has given us superior brain matter to listen, reason, think through an issue, and yet of all creatures we are the most stubborn in our response to his will.

In our text, we see this illustrated graphically as Mark records, "Then Jesus ordered them all not to speak of it to anyone; but the more he ordered them, the more they told it."

Hendriksen observes, "How emphatically the obstinacy and perversity of sinful human nature is here revealed."[14] We see it in children. Mother says to Johnny, "I have just finished baking for the church supper; so, whatever you do, don't eat any of those cookies in that white box." Johnny would never have noticed the white box full of cookies, for his mind was on other things. But now the cookies are an irresistible temptation. The forbidden fruit must be tasted. The sign "Wet Paint" demands we touch to test it.

170

Mark Twain talks of "swimming pools which were forbidden us and therefore much frequented."

Sometimes this is called "the law of reversed effort." When you want certain people to do something, just tell them *not* to do it. How true it is that law makes sinners of us all. Think how many marriages have ended up in divorce courts, how many friendships have been destroyed, how many opportunities have gone down the drain, how many nations have gone to battlefields, because of the sin of stubbornness.

The more Jesus kept charging them not to do it, the more widely they kept on publishing it. What patience our Lord had and what patience our God *has*. It is a wonder our God didn't give up long ago on his stubborn, obstinate, perverse creatures that he made in his own image — a little lower than the angels. But then that is the grace aspect of God's great goodness. He is a God who never gives up. Again and again he calls and we present deaf ears to him and refuse to listen or respond. Like naughty children ignoring the call of their parents when they want to keep on doing what they're doing. "Don't bother me now, Lord. I'm too busy." "I can't hear you, Lord!" "Did you call, Lord? I must not have been listening, Lord!" But God keeps on calling. What a Lord!

One of my students tells of visiting his grandparents. In the morning his grandmother asked him to mow the lawn. He agreed, but one thing after another came up — more important things to occupy his time. His grandmother asked him again and again throughout the day, but he would answer he would do it right after the ball game on television, or after he had called Harry on the phone. After she had asked him several times more, he finally dropped what he was doing and mowed the lawn.

That night he overheard his grandfather say to his grandmother, "How do you have the patience to tell that blockhead twenty times to mow the lawn?" And he heard his grandmother answer, "Well, if I would have told him just nineteen times, all my effort would have been in vain."

Maybe that is the way it is with God. In his infinite wisdom and obstinate optimism, he is determined to save us despite ourselves. As one of my students said in his sermon, "The secret of the salvation of sinners is that God is more stubborn than we are!" Perhaps stubborn is not an acceptable label to place on the love of God, but he is presented to us as the shepherd who searches for the lost sheep until he finds it, and as the old woman who sweeps, and crawls, and feels every corner of her house until the lost coin is located. Being the kind of persons we are, it is fortunate for our own faith that we have such a God and the message of his stubborn determination is the good news of the Gospels again and again.

He Came To Our World — Used Our Language

It needs to be added that although the crowd was wrong in what they did, they were not wrong in what they said. True, they talked when they should have kept their mouths shut, but what they said was true. "How well he does everything!"

It is interesting to note that the injunction Christ gave to the people not to talk about this miracle describes "proclamation," the technical designation for preaching the gospel. Mark says they "proclaimed" the miracle. What the crowds said was right. Christ does all things well.

He still makes the deaf to hear, for we see a parallel in this miracle story to our own experience with Christ. God entered our world and adapted himself to the symbols and language that we could understand. He took on flesh and became one with us. He called us aside in our baptism and personally brought us to stand before his cross. There at Calvary he communicated to us in a language every person could comprehend. A criminal's cross of wood, darkness at noonday, nails driven into human flesh, a thorn-crowned brow, suffering, agony and pain, desertion, and betrayal, and, finally, death.

An old monk announced that he was going to preach on the love of God. When during evening vespers the time came for the sermon, the old monk walked to the chancel. He waited and watched as the last rays of the setting sun filtered through the great stained glass windows and danced a finale of colorful patterns upon the stone of the cathedral floor, and then faded away. Turning to the altar he took the great candle that stood there and held it so that its single circle of light fell on the nails driven into the feet of our

Lord. He lifted the light until it fell upon the spear-torn side. Then he moved it to the hands pierced and held fast to the wooden cross-beam. Finally he held the light so that it flooded the thorn-crowned brow of our Savior. Reverently he lowered the light to the altar, turned and pronounced the votum. His sermon was finished.

So God speaks to us in the language of sign and symbol. And when our ears are opened by this daring deed done for us, then he speaks the words, "It is finished." This is our Ephphatha. For what was finished was not his life, but the work of our salvation. The words, "It is finished," mean for us, "Be open!" and suddenly the Kingdom of God is opened to us. The wall separating God and his people is torn open and the heart of God laid bare for all to see — and it is a father's heart of compassionate love and forgiveness for us all. Easter and the open tomb confirm our openness to God and God's openness to us.

Spittle And Touch

Christ continues to speak to us through the signs and symbols of our own language. The beauty of stained glass, the graceful shapes of carved stone, the thrilling sound of a mighty organ and a well-trained choir, a cross, candles, a table of stone, the color of paraments and robes — this is the language of our world that touches our senses — seeing, hearing, feeling. And they prepare us and communicate to us that God is about to open our ears once more to his word of forgiveness and love. Never underestimate the physical structure of the church building in which we worship. We are an earthly people and God prepares us with the symbols of our earthliness.

But of even greater importance and significance are the sacraments given to us — earthly elements of our world. As he used spittle and touch to assure the deaf man of his concern and cure, so our Lord uses water and wine when he comes to us. Water splashes and runs from the forehead of a baby at the font and a new life noisily enters into the Kingdom of God. Bread and wine touch our lips and suddenly we are opened to the forgiveness and love of God. The sacraments are our "spittle." They speak to us in our language symbols. They work a miracle of new life in us each time

173

we stand before the font and kneel before the table. They are our gestures of grace, receiving, breaking, blessing, giving, kneeling, rising, accepting, carrying the message of forgiveness out to others. In all of this, our ears are opened and we hear, "Given for *you!*" "Shed for *you!*" "Baptized into his death! Raised again!" And we are opened to a new life. Ephphatha! Ephphatha!

1. William Barclay, *And He Had Compassion* (Valley Forge: Judson Press, 1976), p. 66.

2. Marion M. Scott, *Beethoven*, p. 49.

3. Philip Carrington, *According to St. Mark* (London: Cambridge University Press, 1960), p. 159.

4. Alan Richardson, *The Miracle Stories of the Gospels* (London: SCM Press, 1959), p. 84.

5. Ronald S. Wallace, *The Gospel Miracles* (Grand Rapids, Michigan: William B. Eerdmans Publishing Company, 1960), p. 120.

6. William Hendriksen, *Exposition of the Gospel According to Mark*, New Testament Commentaries (Grand Rapids: Baker Book House, 1975), p. 303.

7. *Ibid.*, p. 305.

8. Van der Loos, *The Miracles of Jesus* (Leiden: E. J. Brill, 1968), p. 328.

9. Barclay, *op. cit.*, p. 67.

10. Van der Loos, *op. cit.*, p. 320.

11. R. C. H. Lenski, *The Gospel Selections of the Ancient Church* (Columbus, Ohio: Lutheran Book Concern, 1936), p. 757.

12. Henry Barclay Swete, *The Gospel According to St. Mark* (Grand Rapids: William B. Eerdmans Publishing Company), p. 161.

13. Barclay, *op. cit.*, p. 67.

14. Hendriksen, *op. cit.*, p. 305.

Mark 10:46-52   Proper 25
                                                Pentecost 23
                                            Ordinary Time 30

Miracle 9

The Man Who Shouted So Loudly The Kingdom Came To Him

Bartimaeus, Blind Beggar Of Jericho

Luke 18:35-43; Matthew 20:29-34 *(parallel texts)*

This is the story of a man who shouted so loudly the Kingdom of God came to him. He was blind to the world about him, but not to himself. He saw his own need and faced the helpless desperation of his condition. He knew that, if he were to be cured, help must come from a Messiah sent from God. Isaiah had promised that a savior would come, born of the house of David. And his coming would be marked by the miracle of blind eyes being opened. This promise was Bartimaeus' only hope. He saw that vision of the one who would come more clearly than all the people about him who had two good eyes.

The Messiah came to the city where Bartimaeus sat and begged by the gate. Jesus, on his way to the Holy City, led a parade of his followers to the place of his passion. Ahead of him was a coronation of death. His crown would be made of thorns and his throne would be a criminal's cross. The decisive hour had struck. The Messianic secret was out. No longer would he be reluctant to show all people what it really meant to be the true king of Israel. Then irony of ironies, the first man to recognize and hail him king was a blind man.

Here we see the great storyteller Mark at his best. He paints the character of Bartimaeus in such vivid and striking details that Jesus almost fades into the background so far as the drama of the

175

event is concerned. The spotlight is directed and focused on the blind beggar of Jericho. He is thrust forth in a barrage of strong actions descriptive of quickness, boldness, stubbornness, impetuosity, confidence. Bartimaeus is pictured as quick to grasp the opportunity to be healed — bold in his use of the title "Son of David" — stubborn in his refusal to be silenced — *impetuous* in his readiness to throw aside his garment and come to Jesus — *confident* in his loyalty to follow Jesus to Jerusalem. The whole account bristles with excitement and expectation.

Discipleship As A Divine Miracle

At first this miracle might appear as just another healing of a blind man, but it is so much more. Edward Schweizer in *The Good News According to Mark* titles his treatment of this miracle "Discipleship as a Divine Miracle." He states, "This story has been placed here by Mark, who transformed it into a picture of discipleship by the addition of the last few words."[1] For Schweizer it is a miracle of enlightenment; it is not just a story about how one man's eyes were opened but about how all persons' eyes might be opened to the meaning of true discipleship. He continues, "Once more, immediately before the Passion narrative, Mark demonstrates to his readers what faith is and what it means to be a disciple of Jesus."[2] Nineham agrees with Schweizer and sees Mark using this miracle story "as a vehicle for instruction on certain aspects of Christian discipleship."[3]

Here in this simple street drama we see the ten decisive steps to discipleship. The miracle actually reads like a theatre program setting forth each separate act in the process of becoming a follower of Christ. The plot of the story is directed to the disciples and to us. To the disciples this miracle is a parable pointing up the whole meaning and purpose of our Lord's ministry. He so desperately desired that the eyes of his disciples, like those of the blind beggar, would be opened to who he was and why he had come into the world.

To us its plot is a parable presenting the true way to discipleship. The points of the parable are obvious by analogy. We sit helpless in our blindness and poverty by the side of the road, while life passes us by. Then Jesus comes. In our wretched desolation and darkness we cry out, "Oh, God, have mercy upon us!" The clamor of the world attempts to drown out our litany for help. But nevertheless Christ hears. He stops. He calls us to him, and as we come his compassion comforts us and cheers us — for his word to us is a word of salvation. Our eyes are opened and we follow him.

In all of Scripture there is no more dramatic and compact picture of what it means to become a disciple of Christ. Therefore a thorough study of this miracle, and the ten steps to discipleship which it contains, is well worth our attention. But before we begin that study, a few exegetical items need to be recalled.

Three Accounts

The Gospels contain three accounts of this miracle. Matthew differs considerably from Mark and Luke in his mention of two blind men. Some scholars hold the opinion that Matthew is talking about a different healing event altogether. Others suggest there were two blind men and Mark and Luke mention only the principal one. Luke places the healing at the entry into Jericho, while Matthew locates the miracle as Jesus is leaving the city. This suggests the possibility of two healings. Van der Loos concludes from his study of these three accounts that "all attempts to bring the stories into line with one another are open to dispute, so that no satisfactory solution can be found."[4]

Jericho

The miracle takes place at Jericho, one of the most ancient cities in the world. It lies about seventeen miles from Jerusalem and some six miles from the river Jordan, controlling some of the most important fords of the river. That may be the reason the invading Hebrews in the time of Joshua felt it was the key fortress which must be overcome before they entered the hill country of Canaan.

The dramatic capture of Jericho is one of the most familiar and favorite stories of the Old Testament. Joshua's army did not mount an attack against the city but marched around it. For six days the priests led Joshua's warriors once each day around the city; on the seventh day, after marching around the city, the priests blew the trumpets, all the multitude of Israelites shouted, and the walls of Jericho came tumbling down.

The parallels of this ancient story to the miracle of Bartimaeus are interesting. In both there is persistence, shouting, and the falling of walls. Bartimaeus, like Joshua, persisted in his attempts to capture something important in his life. For Joshua it was a city; for Bartimaeus it was his sight. And like the trumpets of the priests and the cry of the multitude, Bartimaeus shouted and the scales of his blindness fell from his eyes like the tumbling walls of Jericho. And, we might add, like Joshua, Bartimaeus was able to enter into a new land of promise. When his sight was restored, the blind beggar rose up and followed Jesus.

It is also interesting that Jericho was known as the "city of palms," and the setting of this miracle in the life of our Lord is a prelude to Palm Sunday with our Lord's triumphal entry into Jerusalem. Jesus, like Joshua, was about to attack a key fortress in the form of a cross which had to be overcome before he could enter into the new age of the resurrection. The shadow of the cross, the blare of trumpets, the distant rumble of tumbling walls permeate the miracle with a sense of destiny and place it firmly into the total story of God's mighty acts.

Son Of David

When Bartimaeus calls out to Jesus, he uses the term "Son of David." Josef Schmid points this out as "the first and only time in Mark's Gospel that Jesus is addressed by the title Son of David."[5]

Some scholars, such as Lane, do not believe that Bartimaeus was recognizing Jesus as Messiah. His interpretation is that "all that is required by the ensuing narrative is that the blind man recognize Jesus as the one from whom he could expect the gracious mercy of God."[6]

Hendriksen expresses the opinion of most interpreters when he writes, "Though there are those who deny that Bartimaeus is using the term in the Messianic sense, the probability is that he did so intend it for ... it is clear that during Christ's ministry on earth 'Son of David' and 'Messiah' had become synonyms."[7]

178

Nineham sees this as "the first public and unrebuked recognition of Jesus as Messiah."[8] Up to this point only the demons and the disciples had recognized him as such, and they had been forbidden to speak of it. Now the messianic secret is out and amazingly it is a blind beggar who sees who he really is.

Van der Loos finds the striking point of this miracle in the fact that "Jesus does not reject the title 'Son of David'; his command that the blind man be called rather implies that he pays it particular attention." He continues, "The healing of the blind man who then follows Jesus, on the one hand manifests without any concealment the Messianic glory of Jesus and his pity on those who believe in him, and on the other it characterizes the blindness of the people Israel, whose eyes remain closed to his glory."[9]

Perhaps it should be noted that Jesus in this account makes no claim to be the Son of David; he simply accepts the title from another.

Ten Decisive Steps To Discipleship

We have pointed out that we have here not simply the account of how a blind beggar from Jericho was given his sight, but a profound insight into how to become a disciple. Therefore let us examine each of the decisive steps to discipleship which this miracle story presents.

Step One: "When he heard."

The first step to discipleship begins with a word. Mark says, "When he heard that it was Jesus." This is the beginning not only of faith and discipleship but of all revelation. John introduces his Gospel, "In the beginning was the Word." This is where it all starts — with a word. How many people sit by the side of the road in quiet desperation while life passes them by because no one takes the time, or puts forth the effort, to tell them about Jesus passing by.

An elderly gentleman came into the church office after attending the morning service and announced he wanted to join the church. When he was asked if he had ever been a member of any other church, the man said, "No."

"How long have you been saved?" the pastor asked.

179

"All my life," the man quickly answered.

"Then why have you waited so long to join a church?" the startled pastor inquired.

"Well," the elderly man replied, "no one ever told me about it till this morning."

We do not know who the person was who first told the blind beggar about Jesus. It might have been a friend, or a camel driver taking his caravan into the city, or a pilgrim on his way to Jerusalem. But we do know that there would have been no miracle that day in Jericho without a word spoken by some unnamed witness, or as Spurgeon, referring to this act of witnessing, called it, "A very short sermon that was preached to him."[10]

We may never be chosen by God to play a starring role in his plan of redemption, but we are all called to bear witness to the word — to gossip about the good news of the gospel. And that is vital; for without such testimony no miracle can happen.

Step Two: "He yelled."

The second step in the drama of discipleship is the cry of Bartimaeus, "Jesus! Son of David! Have mercy upon me!" The King James version says, "He begins to cry out." The Good News version says, "He began to shout." Perhaps it would be better stated, "He yelled!" or "screamed!" for the Greek word used here implies a loud, piercing tone like that of an enthusiastic fan at a football game. It was as if his whole life's breath were exploding in a last desperate effort to be heard.

We have said that the blind beggar's cry was initiated by the power of a word someone had shared with him concerning Jesus. And it was more than likely true that behind his yell there was also the remembered instruction of his rabbis in the synagogue who taught him about the coming of the Messiah — the Son of David. He would be the light of the nations and open the eyes of the blind. Bartimaeus' expectations therefore were intense. How he wished he could seek Jesus out, but it was impossible for one imprisoned to a beggar's mat. All he could do was sit and wait — hoping that someday Jesus would pass his way.

Every time he heard a crowd of people approaching, his heart throbbed in his breast. Maybe this was it. And he would cry out into the darkness that surrounded him, "Jesus, Son of David!" But it was only a caravan of merchants coming down from Jerusalem, or a group of pilgrims on their way to a feast at the Temple. How many times had he cried out in vain? How many times had he been disappointed? We can only speculate. But one day his persistence paid off and his cry was heard. Spurgeon puts it, "The blind beggar with but one sermon, and that exceedingly brief, never leaves off praying till Christ grants him his desire."[11]

Is this not true of all our faith encounters and all vital religious experiences? There are no formulas that can be given. No quick and easy solutions. No setting or circumstance that can be artificially created to make the Holy Spirit work. Rather, it is a delicate balance of timing that makes the moment right. No one knows the day or the hour when Christ shall come in Glory, nor do we know the day or the hour when Christ will encounter us personally, and make of what is now only a hope in our hearts a glorious experience for our whole being.

It is not enough to say that we do not find God, it is God who finds us. We need to add that the moment of his finding us cannot be planned, or pre-arranged, or manipulated either by our faith or pious performances. It is something that happens when it happens. It is pure mystery.

Some people think that the church is the place, and prayer the activity, in which God encounters us. Others say it is in the Word that God seeks us. Still others, on sound biblical evidence, state it is in the needs of our fellow humans that God comes to us. But the truth is, none of these is an automatic and absolute key that, like an ignition switch, will instantly turn on the motor and produce an immediate encounter with the living God. The Spirit blows where and when he wills. Most important is not where and how we encounter God, but our sensitivity, alertness, and readiness *to be* encountered by him at any time.

The church, prayer, the Word, and Christian service all enable us to maintain our spiritual sensitivity. However, they are not guarantees. Like the blind beggar Bartimaeus, we will cry out into the darkness again and again, and we will be disappointed again and again. Like Bartimaeus, also, we must not give up, but keep on shouting, "Jesus, Son of David." For as certain as Christ came to Bartimaeus, so he will come to us. When the time is right he will touch us. Then all we long for, and hope for, and search for will be given us.

Step Three: "Many scolded him."

The third step to discipleship is accepting the negative and often hostile reaction we may experience from the world about us. Mark says, "Many scolded him and told him to be quiet." Many reasons are suggested by preachers and scholars to explain the reaction of the crowd.

Spurgeon believed the crowd was motivated by the Devil himself. In his sermon he refers to Diabolus in *Pilgrim's Progress* who has a castle by the gate of mercy, and from this castle shoots at all who seek entrance. He also keeps a big dog that barks and howls and seeks to devour every person who knocks at the gate of mercy. Then Spurgeon proclaims, "Whenever a sinner gets to mercy's gate and begins knocking, that noise is heard in hell, and straightway the devil endeavors to drive the poor wretch away from the gate of hope."[12]

Some scholars suggest that the reason for the crowd's reaction was *fear*. Nineham points out that Jericho was later the seat of a great Roman garrison, and the city was frequently teeming with soldiers.[13] Knowing that Rome had a ruthless reputation of retaliation against rebels, the people were afraid that political overtones would be heard in the blind beggar's yells hailing Jesus as the Messianic King of the Jews. As Barclay points out, "This was a time of strain and tension."[14] The roads were crowded with pilgrims, and rumors were flying everywhere that "the hour" so frequently spoken of by Jesus was about to strike. In the air was a sense of decisive destiny which was both thrilling and frightening.

This political implication seems to be confirmed by the contrast between the name quoted by the crowd and that used by Bartimaeus in his cry. The crowd used the harmless description

"Jesus of Nazareth," but Bartimaeus cried out the politically dangerous title, "Son of David."

We have many "afraid" people in our churches today. They are afraid of too much emotion and shouting too loudly the name of the Lord. There are no Roman soldiers waiting to arrest us, but our friends and neighbors might think that having found salvation we have lost our sanity. Or they might associate our enthusiasm with the radical actions of that strange group of "oddball faith-freaks" in the storefront church down the street. Then, too, we might step on someone's toes or offend a generous supporter of the church. It is much safer never to mention religion or politics in public — particularly in a mixed crowd where strong convictions could create a nasty conflict. Faith is best kept a strictly private affair. It is safer that way.

A young man from a devout family went off to study at the state university. In church circles, the university had the reputation of being a hot-bed of radicals, atheists, and "pinkos." His parents were naturally concerned that their son's Christian faith might be destroyed by the vicious attacks of atheistic professors and student "fellow-travelers."

When he returned home for his first vacation, his parents asked him if his Christian faith had gotten him into trouble with his professors and friends.

"No," the young man casually replied, "nobody knows about it yet."

A light securely hidden under a basket is in little danger of being blown out by the winds of adversity. But it provides very little light for the one who possesses it, and none for those about who blindly stumble in the darkness. Faith is meant to be shared.

Dr. Robert Roth tells of getting a baseball glove handed down many times from older brothers. He complained to his father that so many of his brothers had used it that it had worn thin and did nothing to protect his hand from the sting of a hard-flung baseball.

His father wisely answered him, "A baseball glove is not intended to eliminate the sting, but to increase the size of your catching hand."

So with faith. It is not intended to protect us from the dangers and stings of life but to extend the witness of our lives that more and more might share our faith in Jesus as Lord. How often fear prohibits our faith from moving beyond the limits of our own self-concern. Instead of encouraging others to have faith, like the crowd in the miracle story, we scold them to keep their faith expressions quiet.

Another suggestion from scholars is that the reaction of the crowd came from a sense of propriety. For example, Henry Barclay Swete suggests the crowd reaction was: "Why should this beggar force his misery on the attention of the great Prophet?"[15] The eyes of the whole Jewish nation were on this young man from Nazareth. He was their hero who carried with him all their hopes. Ahead lay the Holy City, and he had set his face toward it with determination. It was rumored that already his disciples were vying and maneuvering to secure strategic positions of power in the Kingdom when Jesus assumed the throne. This was no time for a begging blind man to interrupt a man about to proclaim himself King of all Israel. And what's more, his yelling was out of harmony with the dignity of the person addressed.

Certainly this element of the crowd exists in our contemporary congregations. People who think that a thing is right only when it is done right. People who make a piety of propriety. They are concerned only with appearances, to the end that the church might look good. They are so concerned with form, method, and the impression the actions of the church will make upon the community, that they discourage all social action and involvement in the nitty-gritty problems of our time. It is beneath the dignity of the church, in their estimation, to meddle in the dirty affairs of this world. The church should maintain a pure example of "spiritual concerns." We are in the business of saving "souls," not fighting poverty, crime, and corruption. Avoid the risk of radical causes. Play it safe! Don't rock the boat! Don't climb out on a limb for any reason. But they forget it was "out on a limb" reaching for sinners and outcasts that our Lord was crucified.

The most common interpretation of the reaction of the crowd is best expressed by Josef Schmid when he says, "They regarded his shouting as an annoyance."[16] Sometimes this scene is pictured as one of mass confusion, people engaged in many different activities were all converging at the city gate. However, the true picture would be that of an orderly procession of a rabbi with his students. Some were going before him to prepare the way. More followed behind Jesus, listening. The disciples were immediately around him and Jesus was in the midst of them all teaching as he walked leisurely along. Everyone was extremely attentive. The crowd hung on each word he uttered. For, after all, the Kingdom was about to dawn and this young man had a direct line of communication to the Holy God. He spoke with authority, and the closer Jerusalem loomed up before them, the more authority his words seemed to assume. They wanted to hear every word, and this shouting, blind beggar was drowning out the voice of the Master.

Undoubtedly there are many people like that in our churches today. They are concerned only with their own salvation. The cares and concerns of others are only an annoyance to them. This attitude is generally the result of a false view of faith. They believe each person has to work out his own salvation and is individually responsible for his own faith.

When such an attitude prevails, personal belief becomes a competitive activity, and we push everything and everyone aside in order to secure our own salvation from hell. The truth is, as we have pointed out so often in this discussion of the miracle stories, faith is a cooperative experience.

We can only speculate about what actually motivated the crowd's reactions to Bartimaeus. It may have been fear, or propriety, or annoyance — one or a combination of some or all of these. But of one thing we can be certain, such speculation is necessary because it establishes an identification between us and that crowd reacting in the miracle of healing blind Bartimaeus. We then are brought to examine ourselves and see how far short we constantly fall from measuring up to the type of discipleship our Lord desires of us. So often we are more of a hindrance than a help in bringing blind beggars in need to our Lord. Thus we can appreciate all the more the graciousness of our Lord to the beggars of this world and to us, his so-often-blind followers.

It needs to be added that Bartimaeus was not "put down" or held back by the scolding of the crowd. In fact the discouragement he experienced served like water thrown on a grease fire — it only made the fire of Bartimaeus' zeal to be heard flame up all the more. He simply would not be stopped. However, hearing the cries of the blind beggar, Jesus stopped. That is the next step we will consider.

Step Four: God stops!

This step in the process of discipleship is the most surprising and amazing. It is really unbelievable. In his enactment of events which are to change the course of human history and turn the created cosmos on its axis, God stops to heal a blind beggar.

This action shouts as loudly as the blind beggar did and tells us of God's concern for a particular person in need. We hear so often that "God so loved the *world*." Yet the word "world" is so general and universal in scope that it is easy to miss the fact that these words include us — you and me.

With the mail that arrives each day we frequently receive letters addressed, "Occupant." We know that they were sent by the thousands to everybody in general and to no one in particular. Or sometimes there appears in the newspaper an announcement, "The Public Is Invited." Now in one sense we know this includes us, but in another, more decisive sense we have no real feeling of being personally invited. "Everybody" is nobody in particular.

The glory of the gospel is that, even though it is universal in scope, God uses persons to carry his message personally to others. He intends each person who hears the gospel to tell another, so that we are each directly confronted with the invitation to come to him. And this leads us to the fifth step of discipleship.

Step Five: God calls the blind man to him.

When Jesus hears the cry of Bartimaeus, he stops and turns to those who are with him. "Call him," he tells them. And they go and personally speak to Bartimaeus. "Cheer up!" they say. "Get up; he is calling you." Jesus does not respond in general; he sends representatives to call the blind beggar personally to him.

By this compassionate act, Christ is showing that his concern for an individual need is not something different from what he will do on the cross in Jerusalem. Therefore, we dare not separate the compassion of Christ's life from the passion of his death. Both his life and his dramatic death are essential parts of his total act of dying for each one of us.

Sometimes this incident on the road to Jericho is viewed as an interlude, an interruption in Christ's essential task which is to die on the cross awaiting him just ahead in Jerusalem. The miracle of Bartimaeus is a beautiful picture revealing that God's love is big enough to deal with little things. The whole New Testament testifies to this truth. There is no concern, no person too insignificant for God in his compassionate love to bend down to and touch. The glory of it all is that such bending is not bothersome to God, nor is it an interruption in his redemptive work.

The story is told of a shipwrecked sailor adrift on an angry sea who, in his desperation, cried out this awkward prayer, "Oh, Lord, I've never bothered you before, and if you deliver me from this threatening sea, I solemnly promise you I'll never bother you again."

Such an attitude fails to understand the truth of Holy Scripture that our personal needs are not a bother to God. They are not interruptions to his work. They are an essential part of it. When Jesus stops to heal this blind beggar on the road to Jericho, it is not an interruption in his march to his death. It is an essential event of that march.

The events of Good Friday are often so dramatic and sensational that they blind us to the truth of the cruciform nature of the entire life of Christ. His whole life was an act of dying for others. Like the sun which daily burns itself out for everything in our universe except itself, so the Son of God gives light and life to all the world, and in so doing dies a little with each compassionate act. In Christ, compassion and passion are one. His whole life is cross-shaped. The cross simply brings to a focal point his total life of sacrifice and suffering for all of us — each and every one of us personally. So he sends his disciples to us as he sent them to Bartimaeus with the simple message, "Cheer up! Jesus is calling *you!*"

Step Six: He threw off his cloak.

The sixth step of discipleship is one of the most decisive and certainly the most dramatic. The quick response of Bartimaeus in jumping up and coming to Jesus was a sensational sight to behold. But the spotlight of our attention needs to fall on the cloak that went flying through the air, cast recklessly aside in Bartimaeus' eagerness to get to Jesus. That cloak is symbolic of his total response. This man literally gave the shirt off his back to come to Jesus.

That cloak was the sum total of all Bartimaeus' wealth. In the days of Jesus, among the poor, a man's cloak was his most valued possession. It meant everything to him. Not only was it his only means of warmth against the cold of winter, but for a blind beggar it was an essential means of livelihood. Beggars used their cloaks to catch the coins thrown to them. People avoided close contact with beggars, for there was always the danger of ritual contamination. Most beggars were regarded as sinners and ceremonially unclean. So people stood a safe distance away and tossed their alms. The beggar needed a cloak to catch the coins thrown by these stand-offish givers.

Therefore, when Bartimaeus flung off his cloak and ran to Jesus, he was throwing away everything most dear to him. And certainly this is an important step of discipleship. So often we want to come to Jesus with our arms loaded down with the precious things we are certain we just can't do without. But Jesus cannot fully share his gifts with us until we are willing to come to him as the hymn states, "Nothing in my hands I bring."

A fire raged through an apartment house. From an eighth floor window a woman stood, screaming frantically for help. The firemen raised the narrow ladder to her window. When one climbed up to where she was, there she stood with her arms loaded with valuables. The fireman took one look and cried out, "Lady, if you expect me to save you *and* me, you're going to have to leave all that stuff behind."

It is obvious that we are not stranded in a burning building — at least not yet. It is equally obvious that we are not blind beggars, which means we have more than an old cloak to cast aside if we

188

are to forsake all to follow Jesus. Nevertheless, this step of discipleship will someday be demanded of us all.

Christ does not ask us immediately to denounce the world with all its comforts and advantages when we respond to his call of discipleship. He does not expect us to sell or give away all that we possess and apply for membership in the closest monastery. But he does call us to reevaluate all the things of our lives, and be willing to give up anything that prohibits us from living a life of loving obedience to God our Father.

God created this world and called it "good." He made us stewards of the "stuff" of this world. He expects us to use all we have been given to his glory. He wants us to enjoy the fruits of the earth, to prosper and celebrate with the things of this world. But when the time comes for us to leave behind this world and answer God's call into a new experience of discipleship in another and better world, then we must fling aside our prized possessions with the same joyous abandonment as Bartimaeus when he threw aside his cloak and ran to Jesus.

Step Seven: Jesus asked, "What do you want?"

This is perhaps the strangest step to discipleship. God asks, "What do you want me to do for you?" There is no doubt Jesus knew that Bartimaeus wanted his sight. Still, he asked. Why? Why does God want us to ask him for things he already knows we want and need?

One answer is that this is the means by which he draws us closer to himself, in order that we can become a part of his continual process of making us into the persons we were intended to be. When you bring a little boat up to the dock and throw out the line, so that it encircles a piling and thereby enables you to draw your boat tightly against the dock, you are not creating your own security. You are simply connecting to the security and stability of the dock.

When we ask God for something and so verbalize our needs, we are throwing out a line whereby he might draw us closer to himself. This is true of all prayer. Prayer is the connecting link

189

formed between God and ourselves whereby his strength and stability can become ours. We may think we are doing something important when we pull that rope. It is the dock, however, that is important. For if it were not secure, all our efforts would be in vain and we would be fastening our lives to floating straws.

God, in his kindness, lets us do something, even though he has done everything. He lets us pull on that rope, and pray our prayers, even though the full truth is that the strength we need to pull and to pray comes from him.

Step Eight: Bartimaeus asks for the most!

The eighth step of discipleship calls for reckless courage. Bartimaeus was not timid; he was presumptuous. He asked for the most! When Jesus says, "What do you want me to do for you?" Bartimaeus shouts out, "Teacher, I want to see again!" He pitched his demands high. As Hallmark reminds us that the sender "cared enough to send the very best," Bartimaeus trusted his Lord enough to *ask* the very best.

Bartimaeus may have been blind, but he was no fool. He could have played the role of the humble seeker and started out with a simple request. He could have asked alms of Jesus, in an attempt to gain his sympathy. But he didn't. He came right to the point, "I want to see again."

How many of us have the trust in God to pitch our requests as high as did Bartimaeus? We have strong inner longings for something in our lives, but we are afraid to risk offending God with such sizable demands.

A friend who once served Alexander the Great asked him for some money as a dowry for his daughter. Alexander told him to go to the treasurer and demand what he pleased. The man went straight and demanded an enormous sum. The treasurer was startled and said that he could not pay that amount of money without a written order. So the treasurer went to Alexander and told him that he thought a small part of the amount the man was asking would be more than enough. "No," replied Alexander, "let him have it all. I like that man; he does me honor; he treats me like a king, and proves by what he asks that he believes me to be both rich and generous."

190

So when we pitch our demands high and ask God for the very best, we honor him and prove to him by what we ask that we believe him to be a God both great and generous.

Step Nine: Your faith has made you well.

This is one of the most misunderstood of all the steps to discipleship. Jesus says, "Your faith has made you well." Instantly we settle in on the word "your." Jesus says, "*Your* faith," and this means it was Bartimaeus' faith that was instrumental in the miracle that opened his eyes. Therefore, people do play a vital role in their own redemption. We must have faith. God acts and then we respond with our faith. So we separate the process of salvation into two opposing categories. There is the realm in which God acts; then there is the realm in which we act. Both must be operative if salvation is to be successful.

Now this sounds good. It sounds like what we have heard all our lives. "You have to work to eat." "Nobody gets anything for nothing." "Everything has its price." However, when we turn to the Kingdom of God, such sound advice from the practical world is dead wrong. In the Kingdom, God is the creator and sustainer of all that is. Nothing exists except that which is of God. R. C. Lenski once said, "If God is not Lord of all, He is not Lord at all." Thus even the faith we possess and manifest is a gift from God. We have faith, we respond in faith to God, but we have this faith *from* God and respond with faith *in* God. God gives what he demands in return. What he asks *from* us he provides *for* us.

This exchange should not be too difficult to understand. For nothing we have and possess did we create; it was given to us. We come into this world given a life we did not make. We are naked, defenseless, the most helpless of all God's creatures. We even take our first breath because someone slaps us into a response. We have to be fed, clothed, and protected. We are completely, totally dependent upon others. Everything we gradually acquire comes from others.

The mark of our sinful nature is that the older we become, the more we lose sight of our dependence on others and the more we demand independence from others. Perhaps that is what Jesus means when he says, "Except you become as little children you cannot enter into the Kingdom of God." We need to admit once again our total dependence.

Nowhere is this more important than in the area of salvation. God acts upon us, and then within us. He speaks to us, and then he opens our ears that we might hear the word he speaks. Certainly it is true that we have the freedom to fight and resist the work of God within us; but we can do nothing positive toward our own salvation, for everything has been done for us.

When we are baptized, we are placed in the flowing stream of God's grace. The water of the Spirit surrounds and supports us, and the current of this living water moves us. We can decide to fight God and swim up stream against his will, or we can relax, trust in him, and be carried along in an obedient, buoyant life of joyful discipleship.

One day a little fish heard that fish cannot exist without water. His first reaction was sheer panic. Then he decided he must find water as quickly as possible. So he swam off frantically in all directions asking every fish he met, "Where is there some water?" But the fish only turned over on their bellies, laughing at him. Finally he encountered a kindly, fatherly fish who informed him, "Son, you're swimming in it."

So with God's grace. We are swimming in it. Everything that supports and sustains us is but a gift from God. Hendriksen puts it very well when he writes, "In view of the fact that faith is itself God's gift, it is nothing less than astounding that Jesus in several instances praises the recipient of the gift for exercising it! This proves the generous character of his love."[17]

Jesus says to Bartimaeus, "Go, your faith has made you well." Bartimaeus did not flex the muscles of his faith, and reach around and pat himself on the back, or dash off to brag to his friends about *his* great faith that gained for him his sight. No! He knew who alone had done this miraculous deed that day, and he left all behind and followed him.

Step Ten: He was able to see and followed Jesus.

The final step of discipleship is the most familiar — following Jesus. When Victoria was Queen of England she was probably the most powerful person in the world. One day she said to Gordon of Havelock, "When can you start for India?" Immediately he answered, "Tomorrow." Writers have used this story to illustrate the key to successful and influential lives. When the call comes, great persons are ready — ready to make use of opportunity, or to answer the call of duty.

However, in the New Testament when Christ calls his disciples, they do not answer, "Tomorrow." They say nothing; they drop everything and follow him immediately. Not tomorrow, but today! Like steel drawn to a magnet, men leave all and immediately follow Jesus.

Why this is so cannot be explained; it can only be experienced. The call of Christ carries with it the imperative of immediate reaction. In the Hebraic mind, to hear was to obey. One did not hear the voice of God and then contemplate the pros and cons of following him. If and when you heard the voice of God you obeyed.

It was much like when my mother called to me when I was outside playing. If I did not come immediately, she would come after me. And when she caught hold of me she did not say, "Why didn't you obey me?" Rather she asked, "Didn't you *hear* me?" In her mind, if I heard her I would obey her, because she was my mother. So with God in the Jewish understanding. When God spoke, his word did not assume consideration of a response; it *created* the response, because he was God the Father.

So as soon as Bartimaeus was able to see, he followed Jesus as a spontaneous reaction of sheer joy and grateful enthusiasm.

Thus we have the ten steps of discipleship dramatized in this miracle story. It is an impressive list: hearing about Jesus; hoping persistently; overcoming resistance; discovering God's willingness to stop; receiving a personal call; sacrificing of "stuff"; believing in God's knowledge of our need; asking for the most and the best; responding with a given faith; and following spontaneously after Jesus. A most impressive list, but in the light of God's generous grace, this kind of discipleship is an adventure we can undertake with confidence.

Feel The Weight Of The Cross

When we view the miracle story as a whole, there is one more message that comes through to us loudly and clearly. That message is: Christ opens blind eyes so that faith might fully see.

First, eyes are opened that we might see who Jesus Christ is, the Son of God and the Savior of People. He is the long-waited Messiah, the one sent from God to bring lost children back to the Father-Creator and restore all creation to its intended destiny.

The second aspect of the message is equally important: how this divine redemption is to be accomplished. As we have pointed out above, it is not insignificant that the healing of Bartimaeus occurred while Jesus was moving to Calvary and to the Cross. Compassion and passion must not be separated. We need to have our eyes opened not only to *who* Jesus is but to *how* he is to be our Savior.

Being a disciple involves not only *knowing* Christ but surrendering to him and participating with him in his redemptive action. The miracle of healing blind Bartimaeus points out to us that we should not follow after Christ with our eyes closed. We need to have our eyes opened — completely opened to what true discipleship involves.

Paul writes, "For if we become one with him in dying as he did, in the same way we shall be one with him by being raised to life as he was" (Romans 6:5). Discipleship means we will feel the weight of the cross on our lives.

Some tourists were visiting the famous *Passion Play* in Germany. After one of the performances, they tried to lift the cross carried by Anton Lang who, at that time, was interpreting the role of Jesus. "Why must it be so heavy?" they asked Lang. He answered, "If I did not feel the weight of it, I could not act my part."

Discipleship involves cross-bearing and dying. This does not mean that crosses will be erected in our communities and we will be crucified like our Lord on the local garbage dump. No! It means that we are to die with Christ by daily giving of ourselves to others. Every time we stop as Jesus stopped on the road to Jericho to heal a person in need, we are dying with Christ. Every time we take the precious moments of our lives — moments we would much rather

194

spend doing something to please ourselves — and give those moments to help others, we are dying with Christ.

Christ followed the road to Calvary by way of Jericho. He stopped to heal a poor blind beggar. With his cross of passion ahead of him, he still had time for compassion for others. Therefore, in this miracle story, our Lord's message to us is: He is going up to Jerusalem to die for us, and he invites us to go with him. Not all the way to Jerusalem, but simply to Jericho where needy people cry out for help. As we answer these calls for help and meet these needs, we share in our Lord's death by dying for others. And we can look forward with certainty to that day when we will be resurrected with him into a new and more glorious life. Halleluia!

Let us pick up our palm branches and head for Jerusalem. Our Lord is about to mount his throne!

---

1. Edward Schweizer, *The Good News According to Mark* (Richmond, Virginia: John Knox Press, 1970), p. 223.

2. *Ibid.*, p. 225.

3. D. E. Nineham, *The Gospel of St. Mark*, The Pelican Gospel Commentaries (New York: The Seabury Press, 1963), p. 282.

4. H. Van der Loos, *The Miracles of Jesus* (Leiden: E. J. Brill, 1968), p. 423.

5. Josef Schmid, *The Gospel According to St. Mark*, The Regensburg New Testament (New York: Alba House, 1968), p. 202.

6. William Lane, *The Gospel According to Mark* (Grand Rapids, Michigan: William B. Eerdmans Publishing Company, 1974), p. 387.

7. William Hendriksen, *Exposition of the Gospel According to Mark*, New Testament Commentary (Grand Rapids, Michigan: Baker Book House, 1975), p. 419.

8. Nineham, *op. cit.*, p. 282.

9. Van der Loos, *op. cit.*, p. 425.

10. Charles Hadden Spurgeon, *Spurgeon to Meyer 1834-1929*, Twenty Centuries of Great Preaching (Waco, Texas: Word Book Publishers, 1971), p. 50.

11. Spurgeon, *op. cit.*, p. 52.

12. *Ibid.*, p. 54.

13. Nineham, *op. cit.*, p. 283.

14. William Barclay, *And He Had Compassion* (Valley Forge: Judson Press, 1976), p. 73.

15. Henry Barclay Swete, *The Gospel According to St. Mark* (Grand Rapids, Michigan: William B. Eerdmans Publishing Company, 1956), p. 244.

16. Schmid, *op. cit.*, p. 202.

17. Hendriksen, *op. cit.*, p. 422.

U.S. / Canadian Lectionary Comparison

The following index shows the correlation between the Sundays and special days of the church year as they are titled or labeled in the Revised Common Lectionary published by the Consultation On Common Texts and used in the United States (the reference used for this book) and the Sundays and special days of the church year as they are titled or labeled in the Revised Common Lectionary used in Canada.

Revised Common Lectionary	Canadian Revised Common Lectionary
Advent 1	Advent 1
Advent 2	Advent 2
Advent 3	Advent 3
Advent 4	Advent 4
Christmas Eve	Christmas Eve
Nativity Of The Lord/Christmas Day	The Nativity Of Our Lord
Christmas 1	Christmas 1
January 1 / Holy Name of Jesus	January 1 / The Name Of Jesus
Christmas 2	Christmas 2
Epiphany Of The Lord	The Epiphany Of Our Lord
Baptism Of The Lord / Epiphany 1	The Baptism Of Our Lord / Proper 1
Epiphany 2 / Ordinary Time 2	Epiphany 2 / Proper 2
Epiphany 3 / Ordinary Time 3	Epiphany 3 / Proper 3
Epiphany 4 / Ordinary Time 4	Epiphany 4 / Proper 4
Epiphany 5 / Ordinary Time 5	Epiphany 5 / Proper 5
Epiphany 6 / Ordinary Time 6	Epiphany 6 / Proper 6
Epiphany 7 / Ordinary Time 7	Epiphany 7 / Proper 7
Epiphany 8 / Ordinary Time 8	Epiphany 8 / Proper 8
Transfiguration Of The Lord / Last Sunday After Epiphany	The Transfiguration Of Our Lord / Last Sunday After Epiphany
Ash Wednesday	Ash Wednesday
Lent 1	Lent 1
Lent 2	Lent 2
Lent 3	Lent 3
Lent 4	Lent 4
Lent 5	Lent 5
Passion/Palm Sunday (Lent 6)	Passion/Palm Sunday
Holy/Maundy Thursday	Holy/Maundy Thursday
Good Friday	Good Friday
Resurrection Of The Lord / Easter	The Resurrection Of Our Lord

Easter 2	Easter 2
Easter 3	Easter 3
Easter 4	Easter 4
Easter 5	Easter 5
Easter 6	Easter 6
Ascension Of The Lord	The Ascension Of Our Lord
Easter 7	Easter 7
Day Of Pentecost	The Day Of Pentecost
Trinity Sunday	The Holy Trinity
Proper 4 / Pentecost 2 / O T 9*	Proper 9
Proper 5 / Pent 3 / O T 10	Proper 10
Proper 6 / Pent 4 / O T 11	Proper 11
Proper 7 / Pent 5 / O T 12	Proper 12
Proper 8 / Pent 6 / O T 13	Proper 13
Proper 9 / Pent 7 / O T 14	Proper 14
Proper 10 / Pent 8 / O T 15	Proper 15
Proper 11 / Pent 9 / O T 16	Proper 16
Proper 12 / Pent 10 / O T 17	Proper 17
Proper 13 / Pent 11 / O T 18	Proper 18
Proper 14 / Pent 12 / O T 19	Proper 19
Proper 15 / Pent 13 / O T 20	Proper 20
Proper 16 / Pent 14 / O T 21	Proper 21
Proper 17 / Pent 15 / O T 22	Proper 22
Proper 18 / Pent 16 / O T 23	Proper 23
Proper 19 / Pent 17 / O T 24	Proper 24
Proper 20 / Pent 18 / O T 25	Proper 25
Proper 21 / Pent 19 / O T 26	Proper 26
Proper 22 / Pent 20 / O T 27	Proper 27
Proper 23 / Pent 21 / O T 28	Proper 28
Proper 24 / Pent 22 / O T 29	Proper 29
Proper 25 / Pent 23 / O T 30	Proper 30
Proper 26 / Pent 24 / O T 31	Proper 31
Proper 27 / Pent 25 / O T 32	Proper 32
Proper 28 / Pent 26 / O T 33	Proper 33
Christ The King (Proper 29 / O T 34)	Proper 34 / Christ The King/ Reign Of Christ

Reformation Day (October 31)	Reformation Day (October 31)
All Saints' Day (November 1 or 1st Sunday in November)	All Saints' Day (November 1)
Thanksgiving Day (4th Thursday of November)	Thanksgiving Day (2nd Monday of October)

*O T = Ordinary Time

198